THE BEST OF THE BAREFOOT FARMER, VOLUME II

The Best of the Barefoot Farmer, Volume II

Jeff Poppen

Second edition 2021
Published by Jeff Poppen
Red Boiling Springs, Tennessee
www.barefootfarmer.com

The dates at the end of the articles signify when they were first published by the Macon County Chronicle 2000 -2011 and have been substantially revised for this edition.

Acknowledgements:
Editing and Typesetting - Victoria Kindle,
Sally Yancey, & Crystal Justice
Book Design - Victoria Kindle
Ebook Edition - Victoria Kindle
Illustrations - Linda Johnson
Front and back cover photos -Alan Messer
Encouragement - Coree Entwistle

*I'd like to thank everyone who has
helped to make our place a real
community farm:*

*The neighbors and visitors who
drop by everyday,
The students and interns who
stay for weeks or months,
The customers who
live off the farm's produce,
The workers who
lovingly labor on this land,
and especially to my friends and family.*

Contents

Foreword		1
A Note From The Farmer		5
I	Community and the Farm Economy	9
II	Building Beautiful Soil	33
III	A Garden Grows Many Questions	59
IV	Adventures Of A Truck Farmer	91
V	A Garden Needs A Farm	121
VI	What Is Biodynamics?	149
VII	We Can Grow All Our Own Food	189

Foreword

by Hugh Lovell

I met Jeff in 1986, as we were both developing biodynamic farms in the southeast, his in Tennessee and mine in Georgia.

One of the realities we faced was that twentieth century farm policy had consolidated small farms and sent their close-knit communities packing to the big cities. Over the years, the land had increasingly passed into the hands of a few 'strong' but solemnly aging operators, while the larger, more productive regions tended to be exploited by corporations with a short-term, industrial vision that viewed land as a commodity.

Despite our senior status we were youngsters as far as the median age of farmers went. It took us decades to learn the ins and outs of our landscapes, soils, weather patterns, crop and livestock synergies, and how to do things with minimal machinery or investment. In the process we learned to restore our landscapes to fertility capable of regenerating itself independent of inputs.

What was going to happen as the 70, 80 and 90 year olds who made up most of the farm population passed from the scene? How would we fill the void when these oldsters were gone? Where would the next generation of eager, willing hands come from, and who will draw out their talent, willingness and sense of having fun while filling these gaps?

We'd found that to be sustainable, farming must be restorative. What this boils down to is the land needs more people on it to thrive. Diverse and synergistic ecologies are the work of communities rather than a few 'strong' hands. As our age of cheap, non-renewable resources winds down, bigger no longer looks better. What will our new farm communities look like, and how can they return the soils now farmed to the robust self-sufficiency nature provided a mere three hundred years ago?

Barefoot Farmer is one of those rare visionaries who enjoys having problems because demonstrating remedies is creative and fun. Artists, economists, politicians and plutocrats may have lost sight of the fact that human civilization depends on agriculture, but the way Jeff goes about his farming makes it the richest of cultural experiences. He has time to host gatherings and play music with the best of the local musicians—something Tennessee is blessed with. He writes, hosts a local television show, and mentors young people, and in the process keeps things fluid and creative by laughing at his own mistakes. Jeff's brand of cultural rejuvenation flies off the following pages and carries with it the wisdom of why cows are sacred in India as well as how rewarding diversity, cooperation and community can be. These essays not only would make good suggested reading for our nations' high school students and future farmers, but they should be required reading for every ecologist and social planner who styles him or herself as an environmentalist or supports a green agenda.

–Hugh Lovel,
Guyra, New South Wales, Australia,
20th of July 2011

A Note From the Farmer

Ten years and 500 articles have passed by since the printing of the first book, The Best of The Barefoot Farmer. This collection intends to compliment it, although some repetition is unavoidable. I've learned new tricks, refined old ones, and the gardens get bigger every year.

I started writing a weekly newspaper column in 1993, and called it "Small Farm Journal." My editor and good friend, Jim, renamed it later to "Barefoot Farmer," a pen name which has stuck. I can't type, so everything is written with pen and paper, and a cup of coffee, usually first thing in the morning. Considering the proliferation of written material today, I'm reticent to add to the confusion, but I enjoy journaling about our small farm for an hour every week. I hope you enjoy the results.

I remain convinced that small, organic farms can solve many of the world's problems, from health issues, soil erosion, and environmental pollution, to economics, energy use and social justice.

Jeff Poppen

Chapter I

Community and The Farm Economy

    Mission
    Why We Need Farms
    CSA
    Labor
    Price
    Organization
    Local Food
    Letter To CSA

Gardening teaches sharing;
it's a great way to get to know your neighbors.

Jeff

I

Community and the Farm Economy

Mission Statement

Every now and then I review the purpose of our farm, the underlying beliefs and values, the short and long-term goals, and the direction it is going. It's an effort for me to sort out which is which. We are trying to make a living on a farm, to run it organically, and to share the experiences with you. Since we live in a world dominated by corporations, I'll use the corporate model as an outline.

Mission Statement:

Our aim is to grow high quality food and help others do the same, and to educate ourselves on how this is most efficiently accomplished.

Beliefs and Values:

1. Food is healthiest when it comes from a humus-rich farm, which produces its own feed and fertility, and a garden, which is enriched with the farm's compost.
2. The welfare of a community is enhanced when local organic farms and gardens help supply its needs.
3. The care of the soil is the farmer's primary concern, and the marketing of farm products is best done by others.
4. Farms and gardens can be enjoyable, productive and beautiful, while providing meaningful jobs and raising environmental awareness.
5. Community supported agriculture offers a way to sustain such farms and gardens, and an opportunity to distribute fresh produce in an economically cooperative manner.

Goals:

1. A vibrant, community supported farm.
2. The prime utilization of the pastures.
3. The conservation of the forest, soil and water.
4. Providing an aesthetically pleasing place for recreation, education and healing for children, neighbors and guests.
5. Publicizing our experiences through various media.

Vision:

An enjoyable, park-like farm, which remains relatively independent regarding its own food, feed and fertilizer needs, that serves the broader community as an environmentally sound and economically viable model for quality food production.

Now that I've got that out of my way, I'm ready to spread tons of compost, plow and plant six acres of vegetables, keep the cattle moving around the farm, plan a few gatherings, and write another article. But the latter will have to wait until next week.

March 17th, 2008

Why We Need Farms

We need farms for a variety of reasons, besides just a place to get our bread. The domestication of cattle and the dawn of agriculture gave birth to the rise of civilization and the growth of human culture. Much of the work was done by slave labor. As consciousness expanded, hired labor became the norm. Farms are at the cutting edge of a future where people donate labor out of love for their work and each other. As the old saying goes "you don't count your labor on a farm," meaning farmers love their whole lifestyle while not regarding money as the most important aspect of it.

Although the farmer gets just a few pennies from the dollar we spend on our daily bread, the rest of the dollar is widely distributed. Farms create jobs. For every 6 or 7 farms in a neighborhood, one business sprouts up in town. There are lots of tasks involved in turning farm products into food, clothing and shelter. But the farm is the place where it all starts, where the miracle of photosynthesis annually creates wealth from sun, air, water, and earth. Filling needs with the least effort is the true economy. The market economy relies on the productivity of farms.

Healthy farms are good for the environment and less likely to become a subdivision. A farmer's care for the land is reflected in the scenery. A drive through the countryside uplifts the spirit. Instinctively, we still feel inwardly secure when we see crops, animals and the potential for next year's food supply. Local food production consumes less energy and recycles carbon, nitrogen and other nutrients. The diversity of plants and livestock on a farm is mutually sustainable, and good farmers conserve and preserve soil and water as if their lives depended on it.

Farms offer amazing opportunities. A simple lesson like "you reap what you sow" becomes much more real when you've planted the wrong type of bean seed like I did last year. Cause and effect, barnyard animal antics, pond ecology, the continual changing of the seasons, and all of the natural processes happening on a farm teach a morality and practicality largely unavailable in modern education. Willpower and work ethics are enhanced by farm life.

Farms are fun places to visit, for camping, hiking, swimming, hunting and other entertainment. Communities form around farms, with picnics and bonfires, family and friends. A net is created for the less fortunate, handicapped and older folks. Nature's display of interesting insects, industrious wildlife and colorful forests never cease to amuse and amaze.

America stands at an interesting crossroads now, importing most of its food from other countries, and promoting an unsustainable and highly toxic agriculture here. There are more Americans today in prison than there are Americans who are farmers, a fact we would have found unimaginable a few generations ago when the prison population was way less than one percent of the farming population. Thomas Jefferson, among many others, believed that small farmers and small businesses were necessary for democracy.

Farms certainly provide more freedom than other lifestyles, and allow people to supply their needs without the global economy and all of it's social and environmental ramifications.

So, we need farms for economic reasons, for a healthier environment, as well as education, entertainment and inspiration. And we need farms for one other reason – to give us this day our daily bread.

November 6th, 2007

Community Supported Agriculture

Community Supported Agriculture (CSA) has its roots in the recognition of the fundamental difference between growing something and selling it. By juggling around a farm's organic material and livestock, food pours like manna from heaven on this earthly paradise. Plants, powered by the sun, can't help but create food and feed from the air and rain, and each year the animals reproduce. These resources, the farm's cornucopia, are a result of nature. There is more every year.

On the other hand, what happens after harvest is no longer a result of nature or growth. People are involved in transporting, distributing and consuming the farm's production. We use it all up.

These two economies are mutually dependent and make a whole, but work best autonomously. Farmers have no business in the market economy, where excess production creates problems. Farming is a production economy; plants and animals grow as dynamic processes of nature. What's done to the farm's production afterward is manufacturing and marketing; human processes in a reduction economy. Without a clear delineation between these two economies, trying to make money can erode the landscape. Farmers and gardeners have to resolve the conflict of caring for the land on the one hand, with the demands of the community for good food. The earth cannot afford the market economy to continually invade nature.

The health of a community is based on the health of the soil which produces its food. The marketplace has no bearing on the processes occurring on the farm. When farmers can make decisions from the needs of the farm itself, rather than from monetary concerns, farms thrive.

Marketing is not the farmer's forte, just as farming is not for most people. A "farmers market" is an oxymoron. Cooperating is more economical than competing.

Farmers balance the give and take relationship with the soil to both provide human sustenance and sustain soil productivity. When a group of people cover the farm's annual budget, as in CSA, farmers are able to put all their attention into developing the farm's unique possibilities. With the proper amount of livestock, a farm organizes itself as a self-contained individuality, able to offer its supporters an abundance and diversity of food while maintaining its own fertility and capacity for future production. This is made possible by the farmer's skill in handling manure and making compost.

I first heard about CSA in 1987. A group of families took care of a New England farm's financial budget, each giving what they could afford. In exchange, they went to the farm each week and took all the produce they wanted. I love the concept of giving what you can and taking what you need, so I started a CSA the next year. We pre-sold shares of crops for three years, but kept the traditional marketing going, too. In 2000, the CSA really came together, with the members organizing it much better than I could.

It worked. Within a few years we quit marketing altogether, and dropped the organic/biodynamic certification we had for 15 years. Although our practices hadn't changed, certification wasn't necessary anymore. After eight seasons, members still pay the same, $15 to $25 per week, and can come inspect the farm themselves. No longer are vegetables washed, packed, and brokered – they're simply harvested into bushel baskets and sent to Nashville every week, where the members drop by and pick up what they want. CSA allows us to grow the highest quality produce we can, and provides the easiest access of fresh food for the members. Freed up now to focus solely on farming, the harvests have been astounding and steadily increasing. Friends and neighbors of the members get free produce, three charity groups get all the excess, and we continue to supply several smaller CSA's with the extra winter squash, greens and potatoes.

We don't get paid for just vegetables anymore; our job is to run a farm and have the ground ready for the next crops. This involves cutting and baling hay, building fences, liming meadows, intensively grazing cattle, managing wetlands and forest, and making the biodynamic preparations to go into the compost piles. These activities are integral to growing a garden that will thrive despite erratic weather, but gardening is just one part of the whole farm. I take my cues from the farm's needs and Mother Nature, who are much wiser bosses than the marketplace.

The members also enjoy other farm benefits besides the garden produce. They have an open invitation to hike around their farm, picnic, swim, or camp out. By supporting the whole farm, they know what their food dollars are doing. These new friends are reestablishing a direct connection to a piece of land, reuniting a lost tie between city and country, and consciously creating wealth and better health in the local environment. I'd like to call this a revolutionary new food distribution system based on human trust and care of the soil, not profit. But it's not new; it's the ancient tradition of the land's bounty benefiting the community which supports the farmers, the livestock and the soil. Becoming part of a farm and rekindling this feeling of caring for the land may be more nourishing than the fresh food the members get each week.

December 18th, 2007

Conversations with Hartmut von Jeetzee and Traugher Groh contributed vital ideas expressed in this article.

Labor

I just read Anna Karenina, by Leo Tolstoy, and his thoughts on farm labor echoed my own. The laborers themselves are the chief elements to be studied and taken as a governing factor in the choice of agricultural methods. No sort of activity will be lasting that is not based on their self-interest. Human labor plus the products and processes of nature create wealth. Nature by herself creates less wealth than when humans add labor.

Improvements in labor, such as farm machinery, undermine culture if they don't incorporate the laborers. Stimulating the development of industry arrests agricultural progress and the safety net of the community that small, independent farms foster. An appropriate amount of machinery and industry can be beneficial, but an excess can impair the health of the environment, cause unemployment and create conditions that ignore basic human needs. The most important aspect on a farm is the people.

We are dependent on the land for our daily food, and consequently dependent on farm labor. When farms produce a variety of agricultural products, a local culture is developed. When they don't it disappears, taking with it a healthy social network.

As I grew up in the rural Midwest, diversified small farms became large monoculture agribusinesses. Farmers were encouraged to get rid of their livestock and fences, and to row crop immense acreage. This decreased the dependency for farm labor and increased dependency on chemicals, bigger machines, and petroleum. Along with this was the need to import food. The impact of this change is that now America is a net importer of food, so that the wealth created by our daily need for food enriches other countries and the corporations that move food around. Less than 1% of the world population controls 90% of the world's resources, and the 350 richest people together own half of the world's wealth. This disparity in wealth creates enormous social problems.

When I moved to Macon County in the early 1970's, most farms had a garden. These farms had livestock and a tobacco patch, and the laborers were the farmer and his family. Wealth was created locally. A lively local culture existed, arising out of tobacco work and preparing the farm products into the daily meals.

But on paper it did not add up to increasing the gross national product. That's because we ate much of our wealth right here. We did not need money to buy food from somewhere else. I'll never forget those mid-day dinners during tobacco harvest: 3 kinds of homegrown meat, homegrown vegetables, home canned jars of whatever wasn't in season, 3 kinds of pies from fruit from their own orchard, milk, eggs, and everything right from the farm. All of this put a lot of people to work, but didn't show up in the GNP.

The erratic schedule of farm life suits some folk better than the 9 to 5 routine, and the opportunities now for the revitalization of rural America are rising. Farming puts people to work, creates wealth and decreases our dependency on foreign resources. As the people in urban areas ask for more healthy local food, the need for diversified small farms to supply it increases.

Developing industry will create more unemployment, not less. Rural development depends on utilizing our local resources wisely. When the self-interest of the laborer aligns with the best interests of the community, everyone will have a job, good food and a good place to live.

October 19th, 2010

Price

After we've grown a crop, how do we know what to charge for it? The laws of supply and demand can hurt or hinder us. Many a farmer has lost money because of bumper crops and consequently lower prices. Community Supported Agriculture seeks to remedy this ironic situation. A true price for all of our crops is the amount of money I need to grow these crops again next year. The farm's annual budget is paid by folks who get last year's crops. This money must see us through until we get to this point next year. Our CSA members don't buy vegetables from us, they buy a share of the farm's production. I figure out a budget, based on our annual expenses, and the CSA covers it.

Crop failure can also hurt a farm. I'd hate to guess how much labor and expense we put into the 400 tomato plants we watched die this summer. They simply needed a warmer and drier July, which was the coldest on record. Apparently, it was a tomato disaster all throughout the Southeast. We soon had zero tomatoes and many disappointed CSA members. Because we are supported financially by this community, we lost no money. They got plenty of other vegetables, just no tomatoes. If I had been marketing them differently than with the CSA program, it would have been a huge financial loss. Two years ago the sweet corn was weak, but we made up for it in the last two seasons. Every year there are both crop failures and bumper crops.

In an effort to further support the farm, and the CSA movement, we grow extra winter squash and sweet potatoes. Several CSA's get these from us, as they take up a lot of space in the garden. Thus, these CSA's can focus on the other crops. What do I charge for them?

Twenty years ago, I sold winter squash and sweet potatoes for 80¢ a pound, so I still charge the same. A few health food store still get a few loads each year, too. They count on me, and I count on them.

But here's how I like to look at it. I just give away this year's crop. It'll do me no good, except as pig food or compost, besides what I can eat. Whoever I give it to pays me now for the next year's crop. Next fall, I give them their annual load of winter squash and sweet potatoes, and they, in turn, pay me for the following season's crop.

This is an example of associative economics; groups of people working together to ensure fair prices and high quality. These customers know me and trust in my methods and I know them and trust that they'll take our excess.

So we counted out 1200 winter squash and loaded them, along with a ton of sweet potatoes, and sent them to a CSA in North Georgia. 1000 pounds went to a member owned co-op in Atlanta.

The farm feels lighter. It's healthier, too, with money in the bank to grow these crops again next year. We are acting as if there is a future, caring for the soil and the people whose nutrition comes from it.

November 3rd, 2009

Organization

We just picked ten bushels of beautiful tomatoes, on October 25, and the plants are loaded with blooms and green ones. Compare this to last year when there was not one tomato by the middle of August. It makes one wonder about the nature of disease.

When an organism and its environment are not integrated, synchronized or well organized, specific organs in that environment malfunction. Ecological stress disorganizes the stream of life. Every living thing must die. The stage before death we call disease. The ease of living so prevalent in the growing stages eventually wanes and life isn't so easy. Then we have a "dis-ease."

Last July we had record low temperatures. The nights were surprisingly cool and noticeably unusual for that time of the year. I liked it, as my cabin has no air conditioning, but the tomatoes didn't.

On our end, we planted and tended the tomato patch just as we always had. Plenty of compost was spread and the soil was properly tilled. Holes were dug and the plants were lifted from the cold frames and watered in. Subsequent cultivation and hoeing kept the soil loose and weed-free. Four hundred tomato cages were put on and stakes pounded in the ground held them in place. Hay was applied a foot thick over the whole field as a mulch. By the end of June they looked great.

After a couple of weeks of good harvests, we noticed that some plants had grey, moldy leaves at their bottoms, and this gradually crept up the plant. We pulled about a quarter of the plants out of the field, hoping to prevent the spread of a disease. But the nights remained chilly and the tomatoes kept wilting.

This year I was concerned about putting all of this work into another tomato patch, but we did it anyway. The results, using the same methods, could not have been more different. The bumper crop more than made up for last year's failure. Again, because of the CSA model, I did not make an extra dime on tomatoes this year. They got the entire crop, and are still getting them.

This summer our beans failed. My apologies go out to all of the farm's supporters. Something was not organized well between the beans and their environment. All the farmer can do is organize the life in the soil, and then sow and tend as usual. Life arises as organization increases. Good quality compost has organizational abilities latent in the dormant microbes. Cover crop roots are excellent organizers of the soil structure. Proper tillage sets the stage for planting and growing.

But then there is the weather. Each season I can guarantee the customers bumper crops, and crop failures. I just don't know ahead of time which ones. My faith in good farming practices has been bolstered by the unbelievable tomato harvest this year, and next year I'm looking for lots of beans.

November 2nd, 2010

Local Food

Our farm, known for its "local food," is dependent on the whole world, and probably the universe as well. Starlight and moonshine may contribute something. We share air and water worldwide, and quite a bit of dust flies, too. I use Japanese vehicles and Arabian oil. My ancestry can be quickly traced back to European peasantry, and our livestock breeds lived on European farms, too.

But our farm is relatively independent regarding its fertilizer needs, and this is important to me. By composting the excess hay and animal wastes, the soil can both sustain fertility and export crops. Forests, hedgerows and wetlands play a role, too, and we love to grow cover crops like buckwheat and clover. I also use excess manure from my neighborhood. These are not new farming techniques. On the contrary, it's the way folks farmed for centuries. Try to imagine having what you grew each year being your only source of food. Whether your children lived or died depended on what you planted or harvested. Those people loved their land and learned the hard way how to take care of it, or they didn't make it.

Farmers were priests, and the most respected people in the community. Farmers know that crops are grown with forces far beyond their own control. Farming is humbling, to say the least. You walk around the field, take off your hat, and say thank you, Lord. The magic of photosynthesis and growth instills in us a sense of awe and wonder. We don't understand it.

Observation teaches us how to set the conditions for growth, yet it remains a mystery. Soils full of humus and life usually grow pretty good crops, but much of that life is microscopic and unobservable.

So faith is involved. I trust the proper microbes will do their thing if I farm correctly. We hope the weather will be okay, too. And when farming is not a business but a lifestyle, there is love.

Deeds are done out of love for the land, the animals and the community which supports the farm. Our farm runs on faith, hope and love.

We need to be careful with concepts like "local food". If the Great Plains states grow a higher quality wheat, and the Southeast grows better sweet potatoes, shouldn't we swap? Buying only local doesn't make much sense to farmers with thousands of Northern Plains acres and nobody around to eat all the vegetables they could produce. Every farm is a unique situation. I live on what I grow, but I also like coffee and rice, so I try to support good farming practices where these are grown. The world seems to be getting smaller as I grow older.

What excites me now is Community Sponsored Agriculture, where a group of people takes responsibility for a farm in exchange for produce. Our CSA gives us money, and we run a farm. It requires very long-term thinking. The farm, not monetary concerns, guides my planning. I limed this year for better hay next year. I feed the cattle the following year, then make compost, which isn't used until the year after that.

In turn, it fertilizes soil for many years to come. I'm using their money to get the soil ready four or five years from now. The vegetables I have now are free and need to be eaten before they go bad.

This week we sent in plenty of the following vegetables for about two hundred people: potatoes, peppers, tomatoes, sweet dumpling squash, delicata squash, butternuts, pumpkins, sweet potatoes, rhubarb, lettuce, bok choy, apples, pears, swiss chard, kale, mustard greens, turnips, celery, parsley, mizuna, arugula, and a little thyme and sage.

All of this is easy to grow with a bit of labor, the farm's hay, animal manures and tractors. A garden needs a farm, and a farm needs a community. We always have excess, which we offer to neighbors or donate to charities. I don't feel like I sell produce anymore. I am paid to run a whole farm. We don't want government funding, high prices, farmer's markets or a rising demand. All we need are mouths to feed and community support.

September 30th, 2008

Letter to the CSA

We grew too many vegetables again this year. But our friends have risen to the occasion and dealt with almost all of it. As the last delivery of the year pulls out of Long Hungry, we breathe a sigh of relief and gush out gratitude. Thank goodness for all of your support.

The impetus for our work comes from you, the people who eat our food, read the column, watch the show, or visit the farm. Money flows in and out of here, but it doesn't seem to be the reason for the work. We love what we do and would keep farming anyway, although on a much smaller scale. But the economy of scale and the division of labor allow us maximum production efficiency, and your support makes this possible.

Over the last 30 years, the organic food industry has experienced a boom. I could make a lot of money. Instead, I've made a lot of friends. We are developing an alternative food distribution system, and an associative economic model.

Capitalism has within itself its own seeds of destruction, simply because a few people win the "monopoly game." Humans can rise above the pure egoism, the selfish thought of "It's all about me". Not for moral or religious reasons, but purely from economic and environmental points of view, altruism must replace egoism. We can find the way to relate economically when we study the love between a father, mother and child. We can find the way to relate to the environment when we study nature.

Everyone has the right to life, liberty and the pursuit of happiness, and this includes food. Farmers and consumers can cooperate together to the mutual beneficence of both, as we are doing.

So, food is free. It grows on trees and other plants. Some people love to grow it. Other folks do all of the other jobs that help make the world go around. When farmers focus primarily on farm production and are supported, there is plenty of food for everyone. When a farmer tries to make money, trouble begins.

Commodity markets have killed agriculture, because we lose sight of the whole farm and the importance of humus with the short-term goal of profits. On the other hand, community support revives agriculture, because the farmer feels necessary for the long term. All we've grown belongs to the community supporting us; all they give us allows the farm to continue until the next crop comes in. Just like new parents, we are acting like there is a future and we care about it.

You get something besides food from this farm, and we get something besides money. I'm reluctant to name it, because it might be love, and love is scary. It makes me woozy, dizzy and so happy and so sad. When you think of us, we feel it here. We are connected, and that creates happiness. As the last delivery pulls into town, the sadness of our winter separation dawns on us. This year, please hold back the tears. We aren't going anywhere, and plan to bring occasional emergency relief in the form of fresh kale, chard and parsley from under the row covers, along with butternuts, potatoes and sweet potatoes. Transcend the emotions, and know we'll continue to use your support to get the soil ready for another great year to come.

December 16th, 2008

Chapter II

Building Beautiful Soil

Plowing
Tillage
Cover Crops
Compost
The Future
Notes From Underground
Soft and Fluffy
Gardening Without Irrigation

Only plant roots can build beautiful soil,
I can only make their work easier.

Jeff

II

Building Beautiful Soil

Plowing

Plowing is one of nature's mysteries. I plow to fluff up the soil in the spring, but plowing destroys soil structure. This irony is hard to explain but easy to experience. I'll try to explain my experience.

Over the winter the ground gets packed down. A cover crop of crimson clover and turnips, or rye and vetch, or wheat and peas, helps to alleviate the effect of heavy rainfall. But it needs to be turned under so we can plant garden crops. The root growth of the cover crop is what actually builds soil structure, not the plowing it in.

A grass and clover sod is the best cover crop, and is best plowed in the fall with a moldboard plow. The mystery is moderation. Like many things in life, tillage is necessary but too much is detrimental. I want to pulverize the soil just to the extent that what's growing there dies and decays, but still leaves the soil structure, created by the cover crop roots, intact.

I started farming with my dad's equipment, a plow and a disc. After plowing I disced the field. It still had clods. So I disced again and it looked a little better. Another few passes with the disc and the ground was powder. I thought this was good soil structure.

Then it rained. The clay powder and water formed a big brick the size of my garden. I was starting to learn something. I'd seen the same phenomenon after rototilling; a fine seed bed turned into cement after a hard rain. An old timer gave me the clue. "Plow, and then lightly harrow, but don't over work the soil". I threw the disc and tiller away, and got a chisel plow and harrow. The disc and tiller aren't destructive on a sandy loam like my dad had, but they can be on our clay loam.

I learned a little tillage goes a long way. The soil has a life of its own, and when we run through it with iron, this life suffers. We need to plow gently, slowly, and as little as possible, and we must take care to reinvest in the soil biology.

Time is on our side. After I mow the cover crop, I run the chisel plow, also called a rebreaker, lengthwise through the field. The shanks are a foot apart and dig in about a foot deep. This tillage disturbs the cover crop, but certainly doesn't kill it.

My next chore is spreading compost, which has life in it. Microbes in the compost feed on the decaying organic matter from the cover crop and in the soil. After a few days, I'm back over the field with the chisel plow, but this time I go crosswise, so now the soil is cut two ways and the cover crop gives up trying to regrow.

At this point I have a desire to go over the soil several times, completely pulverizing it and making a fine seed bed. But I have learned not to do this, because I want a garden and not a cement sidewalk. I will be cultivating the soil during summer, and this subsequent tillage will remove grass clumps and clods while the garden crop is growing. It doesn't need to be done all at once before planting.

The third and final pass with the chisel plow happens in a week or two, with a section harrow chained behind. The ground still looks rough afterward, but the cover crop is gone, the compost is incorporated, and it's ready to make rows and plant. The finer the seed bed, the more a crust will form, so I try to keep it rough. The life in the soil will soften it up in a way the tractor and tillage equipment can never do.

We do make finer seed beds for crops with tiny seeds, such as carrots, lettuce and beets. But these crops get extra compost and much more intensive hoeing and tending. We are constantly breaking up the crust around them. Nature teaches us give and take, moderation, and tender loving care. We have to plow and loosen the soil, but not so much as to lose the precious structure that holds it together. Life in the soil gives us good tilth, that nice crumbly structure.

We can learn nature's mysterious ways. I just wish it didn't take so long.

May 4th, 2010

Tillage

Soils are built up and made better by grass, clover and other cover crops. They add valuable organic matter, mobilize nutrients and their roots help create good soil structure. A major question for gardeners and farmers is "How do we change what's growing on our soil, and get it prepared for the next crop?" The complicated answer is tillage, and humanity's struggle with this is the history of agriculture. The way we till our ground determines to a great extent how well our gardens grow. To grow crops without irrigation, insect problems or diseases requires soft, silky soil that stays loose and friable. Compost gives us the microorganisms which will propagate and help us, but only if we pay careful attention to proper tillage.

The number one rule of tillage is to not work the ground when it's wet. Take a handful of soil and squeeze it and drop it. If it shatters you are good to go, if it stays in a ball, get out of the garden and wait. Plowing soil that sticks together creates clods that will be with you for years. The second rule is to go slow and be gentle. Soils are alive and need to be cared for like a baby. Love your soil and it will treat you well.

We use five different tillage implements to turn our soils from cover crops back into production. The first is the moldboard plow, which flips the soil over. I mainly use it in the fall, to turn sod. The soil is then left roughly plowed over winter, and the freezing and thawing furthers the metamorphosis of the sod into soil. We don't plow deeply though, because we don't want to bring up the subsoil. Ever so slowly we turn the sod over like we were picking up a sleeping baby. A shovel is the gardener's plow, used to dig up what's growing there. If it's too wet the soil will smear, so wait until it dries up.

Plowing only goes so deep. Eventually a hardpan develops below where the plow reaches. A subsoiler sinks into the ground 2 feet deep and breaks up the hardpan. It is used when the soil is thoroughly dry, and it leaves cracks in our tight, clay subsoil. This allows access for air and roots, and the soil-forming microorganisms. We enlarge our garden vertically by subsoiling and making our topsoil deeper. A gardener would use a pick to loosen up the subsoil.

A chisel plow, or rebreaker, is used whenever we don't want to flip the soil over. It has several shanks with shoes on the ends, which chip the soil when the springs get tight and then release. This stirs the soil up real well. By waiting a few days between passes through the field, the microorganisms have time to help with the breakdown of sod and the formation of humus. Then we run the chisel plow through the soil crossways. The gardener uses a digging fork to accomplish the same goal.

The next implement is the harrow. We use a spike-tooth harrow, to level the ground and seedbed, like a gardener would use a rake. I like to wait a few days, let some weed seeds sprout, and then harrow it again before planting, as this saves a lot of weeding later on.

Our final tillage implement is the spader, a tool from Italy that makes a bed for planting. The shoe goes 10" deep, and then up to about 5" before it flips the soil over. It is excellent for retaining good soil structure and incorporating cover crops and compost into the garden. A gardener would mimic this by double digging, which is removing a spadeful of soil, and then breaking up the lower level and putting the topsoil back on top.

I don't use a rototiller, which beats the soil up too much, creating the illusion of good soil structure. But your nice fluffy soil turns hard after a rain, because the soil particles are all the same size. We'd rather have bigger chunks below, getting gradually finer toward the top, so that after a rain the soil still remains soft and friable.

In a sandy soil a disc works well, but it tends to pack clay soils and create clods. Proper tillage, done slowly, gently and with love for the live soil beings, retains the precious soil structure created by your cover crops. Keep the soil loose so your microbes and crop roots can move around easily and have a good time underground, and your garden will grow great.

Cover Crops

Bare ground won't stay bare for long. Nature abhors a vacuum, so Mother Nature quickly sprouts weeds. Instead, we dress her up in cover crops. This is one of the best ways to build soil humus. Most of our vegetables are in and out within three months, so there's plenty of time for growing crops just for the soil. Since I don't want weeds, I plant cover crops.

Between late July and mid-September I sow crimson clover with a nurse crop of buckwheat and brassicas. For our late- maturing crops, like pepper and sweet potato, I sow a mixture of rye and purple hairy vetch, or wheat and Austrian peas. Since we rotate our crops, after a few years all the land gets the benefits these different covers provide.

The potato field was planted in buckwheat and fall Chinese cabbages right after we finished harvesting on July 29th. A month later we dug up and transplanted the Chinese cabbage and bokchoy into garden beds. The buckwheat was two feet tall, blooming like crazy and full of bees and bugs.

I mowed her down and spread 18 loads of biodynamic compost onto that acre and then re-broke the soil. I mixed up a bushel (50 lbs.) of buckwheat seed with five pounds of crimson clover seed and two pounds of daikon radish seed. This made three buckets of seed mix, each bucket containing about three gallons of buckwheat, a quart of crimson clover and a pint of radish seeds.

I quiet myself. Steadily, I pace the field broadcasting the mix. Each handful covers a swath about 15 feet wide. I become mechanical. With every few steps an arc of seeds spreads into the sky. The seeds raise a tiny cloud of dust as they hit the ground. There is an art to sowing seeds and nothing but doing it will improve your skills. Every moment and movement is just like the last one. I cover the seed with a log drag behind the chisel plow. In gratitude I take my hat off and say thank you, and then look for more bare ground. I find it in the freshly harvested melon patch, and this time I sow kale seed, instead of radish, in rows, so that harvesting it will be easier. The buckwheat and clover are broadcast.

Back in the garden, the cucumbers and summer squash patches are petering out. They are still producing, but not much, and the quality is not as high as I would like. So I mow them down, work up the soil and sow seeds. These patches get mustard and turnips in the mix.

Buckwheat jumps up fast and, in a week, the bare ground has a green dress. In two weeks, underneath its cover, the clover and other seeds have sprouted. By a month, the buckwheat has created a white-flowered garment full of life, and the plants underneath are wishing for more light.

Jack Frost comes to the rescue and lays the frost-tender buckwheat down. Now the brassicas claim the field. Giant daikons, colorful turnips, or a coat of kale, mustard and other greens cover the ground. All fall, the clover hides under these green skirts, and there is plenty to eat. Old Man Winter then lays everything low, except the hardy crimson clover. By late April, mama puts a red dress on but look out, because I'll soon be mowing, plowing and sowing again in May.

August 8th, 2009

Compost

Who invented the compost pile? The first credit goes to Mother Nature. She sees that everything which was once alive eventually gets returned to the earth to decay, turn into humus and help something else grow. But the man who first documented the alternate layering of a few inches of organic matter, manure and soil, and repeating this until a five foot tall heap was formed, was a British scientist named Sir Albert Howard. His book, An Agricultural Testament, published in 1940, launched the organic farming movement. He went to India to teach agriculture and learned from them instead.

Where he noticed a marked decline in the health of crops he always found a lack of humus in the soil. Striving to understand why, he came to the startling conclusion of the role humus plays. A survey of agriculture throughout history provided another conclusion; farming is never sustainable without livestock.

His findings echoed the lessons given sixteen years earlier in a lecture course by Rudolph Steiner, who insisted a farm have livestock and make compost. The plant wants to grow in a soil rich in humus, and compost is the best way to build humus. Besides also stressing the importance of keeping animals on the farm, both of these innovative thinkers recognized the detrimental effects of artificial fertilizers. Howard worked in India, where time and again all farming that replaced manure with artificial fertilizer resulted in unhealthy crops which required poison sprays, but only after the soil humus had been depleted. When the humus levels were brought back up, the insects disappeared on their own. This led to a couple of questions: why and how can we best make humus?

The answer to the first question was found under his microscope. Here he saw mycorrhiza, which are the roots of fungi, or mushrooms. The beneficial effect of the air pores in the humus, by allowing easier root penetration and oxygen availability, was well known. But wherever healthy plants were thriving with humus he discovered a fuzzy white growth on the ends of the roots. This turns out to be a mycorrhiza with a symbiotic relationship to the plant, which means it helps the plant rather than hinders it.

When a soil is low in humus the plant roots, try as they may, cannot get the unavailable mineral nutrients from the soil. Artificial fertilizers are not only incomplete, many of them are so acid that they destroy soil humus. The plant becomes stressed from a lack of proper nourishment and sends up signals for Mother Nature to build humus. Consequently, she sends in insects and disease to turn the plant back into the soil.

When a soil has plenty of humus and mycorrhiza present, Mother Nature does something quite different. The plant's roots grow towards the minerals again, and now the magic happens. The mycorrhiza connect the roots to the minerals and make available to the plant the previously unavailable nutrients. The plant takes them in, grows healthy and sends no signal to build humus, hence no insects or diseases invade.

How do we build soil humus so that Mother Nature doesn't do it with our crops? Compost! All enduring civilizations utilized animal manures wisely. By bedding down the livestock with straw and other high-carbon materials, the valuable animal wastes were absorbed and turned into a highly-valued humus.

Howard developed a composting process in Indore, India and called it the Indore process. By alternately layering high-carbon materials, such as vegetable wastes, leaves, and hay, with high nitrogen animal manures, he was doing what good farmers had been doing for centuries. Plant residues alone didn't decompose well. He found the microorganisms in animal wastes indispensable for making good humus.

Adding soil to the layers proved to be invaluable, too, because of the important microorganisms it contains. In particular he liked to use urine-soaked soil from where the animals were being fed, thus incorporating the humus- forming qualities of the urine into the compost pile. Proper moisture, by watering and air, by turning, create the conditions for the rapid decay of the raw materials and the production of a rich humus. Wherever this was applied to the land the crops grew fine with no chemicals needed.

Sir Albert Howard's discoveries inspired many farmers to make compost and throw away the spray rig. J.I. Rodale read his book and started Organic Gardening Magazine. Howard saw a revitalization of farmland by integrating livestock and making compost, and wrote, "The key to a fertile soil and a prosperous agriculture is humus."

January 8th, 2002

The Future

Good farming practices require that we believe in the future. Our soils are a precious but perishable asset on our farms, and can be improved or impoverished. Thinking in the long term helps. I am now making compost piles which won't be spread on the fields until next year, benefiting those fields for years to come. I choose a spring day when it's too wet to plow, plant or hoe. As soon as it dries I'll have plenty of that to do.

Rainwater is exceedingly beneficial for manure. It helps it to rot properly. If a manure pile overheats or gets dry, some of the nitrogen is lost. We want to save as much nitrogen as possible. The addition of hay and soil helps hold the nitrogen in. It all needs moisture to decompose.

After feeding hay to cattle all winter, a large amount of all three ingredients (manure, hay and soil) are available for compost making. If left to themselves, they will slowly form a nice blanket of humus, but valuable nutrients will be leached out into the water and air. We save these and speed up the process by piling it up.

I set the bucket of the front end loader level with the ground. This takes practice, as none of our ground is "level." So, some soil is added, and this is our source of the microorganisms that help in the decomposition process. In a low gear I inch forward, trying to keep the bucket at ground level. The hay and manure roll up and I lift them and start making a wind row. Back and forth, slowly a mound arises. At first it's hard to know where to begin, but eventually the piles appear.

The base of a pile is 10 to 12 feet wide. The sides are nearly vertical, and I make it about 6 feet tall. The length is variable. After it's piled, I place the bucket on top and wiggle it. Pulling backwards leaves a concave depression on the top. This allows for the collection of valuable rainwater.

I'm concerned about moisture in piles made in the spring because dry, hot weather is coming. A fall-made pile will get plenty of moisture. If possible, old hay can be spread on top, keeping the drying sun and wind off.

The last step is adding the herbal preparations. These are specially made humus products from the plants yarrow, chamomile, nettle, oak bark, dandelion and valerian. When I call compost "biodynamic," it refers to the use of these preparations. I think they help.

It's nice to live for today and be spontaneous. But, in the past, we have always had a future. I can't say for sure that we have a future, but if we would act like there is one, that future will be better.

April 28th, 2009

Notes from Underground

As an effort to understand more about what's under the ground we stand on, I took a three day course in microbiology. It's a fascinating subject. The professor dispelled many myths and inspired a desire to learn more. I have a long way to go.

Soils have many nutrients, but in a form that is unavailable to plants. A soil test tells us what's available, and gives recommendations for how much fertilizer to add. The water soluble fertilizer helps the plants to grow, but it destroys the soil microorganisms. Once we learn their role, we don't want to hurt them. There are a thousand times more unavailable nutrients in the soil than available ones, and microbes can make them available.

In a teaspoon of good soil, 600 million bacteria live. In poor soil only 1 million are present. Around a plant root in a live humus soil, you will find 10 to 100 billion bacteria in a teaspoon of soil. That's a big difference. So what do they do?

Plant roots exude carbohydrates as they grow. This is food for microbes; bacteria and fungi live on it. In exchange for this food, they help the plant to grow. Protozoa and nematodes eat the bacteria and fungi. Bugs eat them. Bigger bugs eat the smaller bugs, and so on.

With all this eating going on, there is a lot of excreting going on, as well. This is full of nutrients that the plants can use. So when your soil test says you need 200 pounds of nitrogen, because you only have 20 pounds available, don't worry. Nitrogen-fixing microbes will supply the rest of the nitrogen your crop needs. The same is true for potassium and phosphorus, and the other nutrients plants require. But the microbes have to be there, and this is the problem. They are destroyed by herbicides, insecticides, fungicides and other pesticides. They are also destroyed by fertilizers and compaction. When we apply fertilizer, the ground water becomes full of the nutrients our crop needs. That sounds like a good idea. But the problem is that it kills the microbes, so when the water soluble fertilizer is used up or leaches out, the plant no longer has microbes to feed and protect its roots. So you have to come to the plants rescue with more materials that further destroy microbes.

We can alleviate the situation by making and applying compost. This is where we grow microbes. By mixing up manures, garden refuse, soil, leaves, rotten wood chips and other organic matter, and wetting it down, microbes are propagated. We can enliven the soil with them and they will again feed and protect our crops.

All farmers used to do this. Cover crops are turned under, farm animals graze pastures, compost is made, manure is cared for carefully, and tillage of the soil is slower and done with lighter tractors or horses. We can't go back to those days, but we can use what those farmers knew along with these new insights that microbiology has to offer. Once we get the biology corrected, the crops thrive.

One bacterium, if it had the food, can propagate so fast that in three days the total weight of its offspring would weigh more than the earth. With life in the soil, nutrients are held, water is retained, diseases can't grow and insect eggs are eaten before they hatch. If the soil needs life, the insect egg hatches, and plants are destroyed in order to give life to the soil. Since microbes are easy to grow, it makes sense to grow them and not let the insects do the job of giving life to the soil.

Different microbes grow around different plants. We want a large diversity of plants so we have a large diversity of microbes. Growing crops with microbiology is the way it's always been done. We have temporarily dropped their populations with chemicals and compaction to the point where crops require fertilizers and pesticides. With compost to the rescue, live humus soils are built which can again grow crops naturally. That's my understanding of the underground.

September 22nd, 2009

Soft and Fluffy

Plowing and harrowing leaves the soil fully pulverized, soft and fluffy. Even after a rainstorm the tilth will remain loose and mellow. If it gets hard, the organic matter is too low and there is nothing to fluff up or there is a lack of biological activity.

The last two conditions are remedied by good quality compost. We ferment manure with bedding, soil, and garden refuse for a year, and apply it liberally on the crop land. Fifty tons to the acre figures out to be about a third of an inch thick, spread over the whole field. A few years of this, along with cover crops, builds up a live soil humus with plenty of organic matter and beneficial microorganisms.

I need to be able to walk in a field and sink down a few inches into the soft soil. I quickly retreat so I don't squish any microbes. Silky, velvety, satiny to the feel, the garden is like a down pillow, impressionable and responsive. Now I can start to picture a crop growing here.

The Farmall tractor has shoes behind the back tires that lay off rows about 45 inches apart. After the first pass, I turn the tractor around and put one tire in the outside row, re-plowing it and making the next row with the other tire and shoe.

The soil must be dry enough to fall apart when a handful is squeezed and dropped, otherwise it will form clods. If soil is coming up on the tractor tire, it is probably too damp to plow. One of the hardest jobs for a vegetable grower is simply waiting for the ground to dry. The calendar says it's time to plant, and the seeds are still in the house.

Instead of working moist soil and planting, we find other jobs to do. I'd much rather plant in dry soil with a few dry days ahead, so I can rake or harrow over the tops of the rows. A prolonged wet spell in the spring means lots more weeds. If the garden is unplanted, I can take care of them with a tractor. Late gardens do great here in Tennessee anyway, so I try not to rush it.

Once the rows are laid out, we drop the seed by hand and step on it. This firms it into the soft soil, ensuring good seed to soil contact. The seeds absorb moisture from the soil even if it doesn't rain, if they are compressed with the earth. I straddle the rows with the cultivators down to cover up the rows with loose soil.

In a few days I harrow over the whole field, being careful not to put the tires on top of the rows. I can follow the tracks left by the shoes behind the tires on the previous pass which covered up the rows. Sometimes it rains and I don't get to do this, and we'll have to get in there with the hoes sooner than if I get to harrow.

When the crop emerges, I like to leave it alone until the second set of leaves appear. The first leaves are called seed leaves, or cotyledons. These leaves nourish the elementary, emerging plant, as the roots are not yet well formed. In a few days the true leaves appear, indicating lateral roots and a good connection to the earth. Now it's time to aerate and check evaporation by cultivation.

On sturdy crops, like corn or potatoes, a rotary hoe or a tine weeder can be pulled right over the plants. The "hoe" looks like a disc with fingers instead of the discs, and they break the crust but don't disturb the crop. Tine weeders are rows of stiff wire that wiggle through the top inch of soil, effectively weeding and aerating. These tools are only used until the plants are six inches tall, and then we straddle the rows and continue to keep the soil soft and fluffy.

May 25th, 2010

Gardening Without Irrigation

Farms well supplied with humus have little trouble growing a garden in a drought without irrigation. A soil with plenty of organic matter soaks up rain like a sponge and can hold it for many months. It's amazing to see gardens thrive with no rain.

A very dry March raised the red flags. If it's this dry now, what will summer be like? Tennessee weather is unpredictable; it can rain every day in July or not a drop. But the drought in March was very odd, so we doubled up on the amount of biodynamic compost for the potato field. Instead of 20 tons we spread 40 on 3/4 of an acre.

I never get to run the subsoiler through the field in the spring, but never say never. A subsoiler breaks up the hard pan, plowing a trench two feet deep. It is only used when the soil is dry so that the clay cracks and doesn't smear back together. This spring it was dry enough to use the subsoiler to help create a lively interaction between the topsoil and the subsoil.

April and May had adequate rainfall, and the compost and subsoil soaked it up. Towards the end of May the spigot turned off, so we got busy. All of the field crops were cultivated and left with a dry, dust mulch on top. The potatoes, corn, and winter squash were hilled. In these instances we are using the soil itself as a mulch. By disrupting crust formation we are stopping evaporation caused by capillary action. The ground underneath the dust mulch stayed moist.

In the garden behind the barn we mulched with hay. Selling some cattle eased the pressure on the farm's grass supply, and several rolls were spread. Most of the spring and early summer crops received a thick layer of hay mulch and produced abundantly.

An inch of delightful rain fell on the summer solstice, and we quickly mulched or cultivated everything we could. It's easy to see why farms need cattle and hay. Cow-power compost and humus-building hay crops kept the fields pushing up the plants, as we worked on the surface, conserving every bit of moisture.

The next dab of rain wasn't till the end of July. To get the fall garden to sprout I used a little trick. Right after bush hogging the old beans, summer squash and cucumber beds we made new furrows and sowed the seeds. Then we walked heel to toe right over the row, firming the seeds in the soil and squishing out the air before raking over them. Normally we don't ever walk on the beds. The beans, squash and cucumbers, with their mulch, have kept the sun off of the soil and left us enough moisture to sprout up the fall crops.

An unbelievably hot August rapidly turned our upper layers of soil into a dusty powder. But the garden did well anyway, with an acre of winter squash producing 500 bushels. These hard squashes withstand drought by sending down a deep tap root, and wilting their leaves during mid-day. The later plantings of peppers and sweet potatoes suffered the most, producing many small fruits and tubers that would have grown larger with more water. The fall garden just sat there in the seedling stage, awaiting rain.

Our delivery van got filled with a thousand pounds of produce each week, but the fall crops were not growing. In early September we transplanted anyway, wondering what would happen. More hay was laid down, and I kept threatening to plow up the awful looking fall green beans. It finally rained an inch in mid-September and everything perked up. Now we're one week into October, still in a drought, but the garden is a sea of knee high greens, keeping 120 families happy. It's an awesome sight.

Let's not forget lime. Calcium flocculates the soil, which means it makes the soil fluffier. Clay soils tend to pack tightly, and lime gets in between the layers and fluffs it up. This allows for better air and water penetration and retention.

Before the advent of commercial fertilizers, market gardeners typically put on 50 to 75 tons of composted manure per acre per year. A full quarter of the garden space was sown in cover crops, as no amount of compost improves soil structure like grass and clover can do. We try to follow these time-tested principles. The potato field had been in white clover for two years, and less than an acre yielded over 300 bushels with hardly any rain.

The ground here is never bare for long. We sow buckwheat in any spot when the crop growing there is finished. Subsoiling, liberal composting, mulching, proper tillage, liming and cover cropping all help to build and conserve the precious soil humus. Thus, the farm can keep producing even when we garden in a drought.

October 2nd, 2007

Chapter III

A Garden Grows Many Questions

Myths
O'ganic
Crop Rotation
Cold Frames
To Plow Or Plant
Weeding
Hoeing
Laying The Garden By
Moon Signs
Pruning
Orchard

I've two answers for most garden questions:
Either "add more compost" or "I don't know".

Jeff

III

A Garden Grows Many Questions

Myths

Organic farming is how folks have grown food throughout history, up until about a hundred years ago. After a few decades of chemicals, a new organic farming movement arose, along with much confusion. I'm still trying to figure it out and sort the myths, with their traces of truth, from reality.

Weeds are soil builders and can be left in the garden. It's true that the wild plants that sprout in our gardens can be beneficial, breaking up hardpan and bringing up nutrients. But one weed in the garden while we're growing vegetables is one too many. Gardening is weeding, and nothing is more detrimental to crop production than weeds. Weeds are only valuable if you are letting the land lay fallow (not trying to grow something), and should not be allowed to go to seed.

Monoculture is bad. You can grow many different crops in the same field. I grew up in monoculture corn and soybean land, and it is bad. We don't grow hundreds of acres of one crop. But many vegetables like to grow in patches. The specific soil microbes that can benefit a particular species wake up and temporarily dominate the patch. I like a field of nothing but potatoes, corn, squash, carrots or tomatoes. It's usually less than an acre, and will be in a different crop within a few months. Nothing but the one crop, monoculture, is a beautiful sight, as long as a rotation of crops follows.

Never use a moldboard plow. By the way, I've tried all these myths personally, and this one really slowed me down. In the spring, soil life wakes up, and flipping it over buries and suffocates biological activity, which is not good. But in a heavy soil, fall plowing can be very beneficial. Incorporating compost and organic matter in the fall gives it time to become part of the soil, and the freezing and thawing of the lifted up chunks of soil helps to pulverize them. We only use the moldboard on sod in fall, and then leave it rough-plowed for the winter to work on it.

Vegetable scraps are compost. No, they can become compost. But until then they are often too long in a smelly bucket under the sink. Yes, they should be composted, but get them outside daily, and covered with dirt, hay, or leaves.

Heirloom seeds are better than hybrids. One of the most satisfying aspects of my gardening experiences is finding and saving old varieties. Our sweet potatoes have been grown nearby for over a hundred years, and we've had them along with our own kale and garlic for over thirty years. Plants become adapted to specific localities and saving seeds is very important work. Although we grow open-pollinated varieties for the most part, we also grow hybrid tomatoes, sweet corn and peppers. Improvements in vigor, disease-resistance and yields simply make them the better option sometimes, and we get no complaints on the flavor of a Better Boy tomato, Silver Queen sweet corn or Carmen peppers.

Rocks and bugs are bad. I used to pull rocks out of the garden and squish all bug eggs. Then I noticed an increase of yields in the rockiest part of some of the gardens. The best looking soil wasn't the best. Some of our best gardens look like they're mulched with rocks. The cottony-looking eggs I'd been squishing were from beneficial insects. The point is to observe carefully; nothing is all bad.

Plant all the gardens in winter cover crops like rye and vetch. By all means, if you don't need to plant the field early the next season. They are great soil builders if left until early May, then mown down and worked into the soil. In a few weeks you are ready to plant a late May crop like corn, sweet potatoes or tomatoes. It takes rye and other grain cover crops two or three weeks to rot. For early crops it's better to leave the land open and roughed up with a chisel or moldboard plow, because it will dry out quicker in the spring and you'll get a head start.

You don't need much compost. This may be true on some soils in some situations. But I look at an extra 20 tons of biodynamic compost as my crop insurance. I use way more composted cow manure than most organic farmers, following advice from a hundred years ago.

Don't cultivate a lot. I till the soil frequently, which is also old wisdom. Yes, the tillage destroys soil life, but large quantities of compost reinvigorate it. A rototiller is the most damaging garden tool there is, beating the soil to death. The cultivators our ancestors used are much better. The more I farm, the more I appreciate the old time methods.

July 7th, 2009

O'ganic

Many new organic gardeners feel the need for a greenhouse, an irrigation system and raised beds, but not for tractors, plows and animals. In this regard, and a few others, I find myself to be more conventional.

Greenhouses are used to start seedlings for transplanting and to extend the season. We simply direct sow lettuce and brassica (members of the cabbage family) seeds in the garden. In six weeks or so they are transplanted bareroot into another spot at about a foot apart. We never transplant squash, melon, okra, bean, cucumber, or corn plants.

Coldframes make more sense to me for raising the tomato, pepper and eggplant seedlings. They are seeded into the ground, not plastic pots, flats or soil blocks. With their roots in the earth they don't require as much watering or other care. Our bare-root plants do wilt at transplanting, but pull out of it just fine. I like the old-fashioned way, it is cheaper and easier than a plastic hoop house. A wooden coldframe with window sashes looks better to me, too.

Our farm sells in-season produce, and I enjoy a break during the winter. The climate here allows many greens to survive until spring under a row cover or two, so we keep a few dozen families happy. If I lived in Maine, I'd have a greenhouse. (It would be made of glass and I wouldn't throw so many stones.)

Building rich soil humus is much simpler than putting in an irrigation system, which we find unnecessary. Spring rains soak into loose soil and remain to water the crops later. I'm very conscious of soil moisture. After every rain I stir the ground as soon as I can to check evaporation and this cultivation creates a dust mulch. All old farming textbooks explain this. In a severe drought we mulch with old hay. Food tastes better if it's not been irrigated.

The idea behind a raised bed is that air is incorporated. I'm a big fan of air in the soil. I like it soft and fluffy, but I'd rather have my crops at ground level, or even sunken a bit, where the ground is more moist. A raised bed will dry out quickly and require irrigation. I like the way they look when used in landscaping, but they're hard to plow around.

A farm needs the proper amount of animals to supply itself with fertility. Cattle give more manure than the crops they eat require, and this leftover manure can be composted and used to grow other crops. This is the basis for traditional agriculture. There is no replacement for animal manure, composted with farm and garden refuse like hay and leaves.

To qualify for USDA organic status, the compost pile must reach 150 degrees. I never want my piles to get over 120 degrees, because I value the enzymes and microbes that are destroyed by overheating. I also don't turn them five times, but would rather it sat undisturbed for up to a year so that fungal hyphae can stretch out through the pile.

To use the word organic now, you must follow rules set by the USDA, which I don't, and you can use materials which I won't. Many organic farmers use potassium sulfate, commercial chicken manure, and fish emulsions for fertilizing, but I believe these products are detrimental because soluble fertilizers harm soil microbes. Good advice is to use your nose; if it doesn't smell good it probably isn't. Any plant-based poison, such as rotenone, pyrethrum, nicotine and many others, is allowed. A poison is a poison and I don't want them on my food.

Dad had a table at the end of the driveway where we offered vegetables for sale. A shoebox collected the money that folks would leave when they got their corn, beans or whatever. It was the honor system. When questioned about people taking without paying, Dad just shrugged his shoulders and said they probably needed it more than anyone else anyway. All were our neighbors, and the farm had community support. That was in the 1960's, and he used the organic method. By the 70's I had my own farm and started selling organic produce. When I took produce somewhere, it was best not to mention the "organic" word. It implied buggy, less-than-perfect vegetables, grown by hippies. The 70's became the 80's and I was still organic. The more I used tractors and plows, the more our production soared.

The 90's became the 2000's. Through all of these decades, I tried many "organic" practices, which I have forsaken for traditional old time methods. I've held onto the word organic long enough. I am now a conventional farmer using practices that are hundreds of years old. Although our farm was certified organic for 15 years, we can't call it organic anymore. We have moved produce without the word before, and now we get to again. I guess I could call it O'ganic.

June 30th, 2009

Crop Rotation

Crop rotations make my head spin. Although I plan and plan about where to plant what crop, the final decision is usually made at the last minute. Many factors are taken into consideration, but ultimately I rely on my imagination. I have to be able to picture the crop at its peak or I'll plant something else.

The fall gardening season begins at the end of July. As the spring and summer plantings peter out, I'm on the lookout for places to plant. Three rows of beets have got to go, and 25 baskets later I have room for lettuce, bok choy and Chinese cabbages. Old onion rows are now planted with cucumbers and sunflowers, and kale is planted where weeds have taken over the basil seedbed.

The carrot rows are now bean rows, and most of the lettuce beds are temporarily in buckwheat, which is what I plant either when I don't know what to plant, or I'm not ready to plant. I have to plant something because bare ground isn't allowed. It would grow up in weeds.

Soon the first planting of summer squash, cucumbers and beans will be history. They'll be mown, plowed in and replanted, probably in fall greens. I'll be wanting to plant mizuna, arugula, collards, mustard and many others in a few weeks. Let's not forget the turnips and radishes either, and we'll need a bed of spinach to overwinter and feed us next spring.

There are a few rules in crop rotation, but we all know what rules are for. It's good to alternate species, and also roots, leaves and fruits. This way the ground isn't sapped of the same nutrients and forces by having beans following beans or beets following beets. Some plants like to follow another plant in particular. Potatoes grow best after clover, but not so well after carrots, beets or other crops that require extra tillage. Nitrogen-loving crops, like corn, love to grow where the nitrogen-fixing legumes have been. Big seeds, like corn or pumpkins, can be sown in rougher, weedier land, unlike the tiny carrot or lettuce seeds. Little seeds need a finer seedbed. But all the rules go out the window if I can't tune in an imagination, a picture of the new planting. I have to be able to see it in my mind.

A good spot for beans is disregarded because of a nearby groundhog hole. The squash here will certainly grow too big to have cucumbers next to them. Next year's corn needs to be where I can put an electric fence around it for raccoon protection, and where in the world will I find a good enough clover patch to turn into a potato patch?

I like a sandy soil for early spring plantings so it'll warm up quicker. I prefer heavy soils for later sowing so they'll hold moisture during summer. Tomatoes need more sun than they're getting this year, and sweet potatoes could follow corn because they don't like extra nitrogen, and corn sucks it up.

I circle around the farm, picturing the crop cycles in the annual turn of the seasons. It's wheels within wheels. Sometimes I get dizzy trying to figure out what I'm doing. Eventually, I'll find a straight row for my seeds to go, and throw my plans of what to sow right out the window.

August 7th, 2007

Cold Frames

New cold frames have sprouted up near the garden and are now full of seeds. Like many new things on this farm, they look old. The window sashes are old, bought cheap at farm auctions. The design is old, too. I remember this style when I was a kid, and it is commonly depicted in old farming and gardening books.

Sassafras boards were cut and nailed together to make eight rectangles 3-feet-wide by 9-feet-long. The backs are 8 inches taller than the fronts, which are a foot tall.

We found a sunny spot in the front lawn and plowed it up. After arranging the boxes we started sifting soil, compost and sand. The sifter is 1/2" hardware cloth nailed to a 2-foot-square frame laid over a wheelbarrow. Leaf mold was laid in the bottoms and the sifted mix filled the frames about 8 inches deep. Into this, we added a little lime, kelp, crushed eggshells and colloidal phosphate. This is stirred in and then left alone.

After sitting a few days, I raked the soil around to disturb the sprouting weeds, and proceeded to plant. Shallow furrows were made about 3 inches apart and tiny tomato and pepper seeds were placed an inch apart in the rows. Small cedar stakes were labeled with the varieties and then I firmed the soil over the rows with the side of my hand and raked dry soil on top with my fingers.

I watered them with rainwater. Rain falls down from the sky, and is different from spring water, which flows horizontally. Well water is brought upward from below. I've heard rainwater is best for plants, and it makes sense, but I've never done experiments using different kinds of water.

We mulched around the south-facing cold frames with rotted wood chips, to keep weeds down. I think the glass and wood look better than a plastic hoop house. If we had dug them deeper and put a foot of horse manure in the bottoms, the composting manure would heat up and they'd be called hot beds.

They'll be kept watered until our seeds sprout. Then we'll have to keep a close eye on them, weeding and watering as necessary. In six to eight weeks we will have plenty of bareroot plants to transplant out in the garden. Every year is a new garden, even when you grow things the old fashioned way. Every season is different, with new failures and new successes. Although organic and local food is now in the news, I consider it to be the good old way.

April 14th, 2009

To Plow or Plant?

The question of freedom comes up when we wonder how an impulse to action arises in us. What compels us can be regarded as necessitated by nature, or as a free decision on our part. To further complicate matters, sometimes we know why we act, and other times our actions surprise us. On the farm we prioritize the things to do, routinely change the plans, and ponder how these decisions come about.

Today I want to plant a half acre of sweet corn, plow land for planting three acres next week, hoe a half-acre of spring crops, and rake over a half-acre of stuff we planted five days ago. It's supposed to rain tonight. So, let's put everything in the right order. If it rains and stays wet for two weeks, which jobs would I rather have done? This thought often pops up as I move toward action. Conversely, I have to consider a possible impending drought. The condition of the soil remains a large consideration.

Getting the corn in, but not being able to harrow over it in a few days would mean a weedy mess. Plowing sooner will help get the new ground ready. Two weeks from now will be late for planting those three acres. Raking over the rows can be done rather quickly and will really help keep weeds down. And all our little plants would love to have their soil tickled to let them know we care and that we won't allow weeds, crusty soil, or compaction to bother them.

It looks like I'll rake first, then hoe, then plow and last of all, plant. This is opposite of what I used to do. I would plant, plant, plant, and then have to hoe weeds. But if I tend what's planted first, hoeing will be much easier as the weeds won't have taken hold yet. If planting gets delayed, it won't be as detrimental as if the hoeing doesn't get done. But I sure would like to get the corn patch planted.

Of course many other factors enter in. People show up, the cows get out, a thundershower comes early, or I walk by the cold frame and decide to weed the little tomato sprouts. No, I can do that last one after a rain, and sharpening the mower blades can wait, too.

If it doesn't rain, what would I like to have done? Again, raking and hoeing come first, because that will check evaporation in the soil. The loosened soil will become a dust mulch and hold in the moisture underneath, keeping it from leaving the ground by capillary action.

Plowing will also conserve moisture, and there'll be plenty of time for planting. Generally speaking, tending what is already planted is top priority. Secondly, we need to get our ground ready for future planting. Lastly, we plant.

Farming is exciting and interesting. So many different activities are involved, and all of them require thinking clearly about how life works in the soil. What is best for the soil microorganisms? Compost. Maybe I could make more compost today. How does one shut the mind off?

Hunger obviously motivates these activities, as does making a living. Beauty plays a role, I like a clean-looking garden. When I supply a good quality product to my customers, I get feelings of doing something important. Which job I enjoy the most doesn't affect my motivations much. I'd rather plant corn.

One other job needs doing today. I'll have to get the weekly article written. I don't know when I'll have time for that. Why do I write it? Perhaps for fame and fortune. Perhaps for the altruistic aim of turning the world into small, self-sufficient organic farms that feed everybody wonderful food and allow for personal freedom.

Guess I'll just go hoe and continue to watch my mind ramble on.

May 29th, 2008

Weeding

You have to work a garden, and the sooner you get the hoes and rakes out, the less work it will be. Don't be fooled by bare ground, it won't stay that way for long. Weeds are sprouting underneath as I write this. Nature loves to grow plants and there are plenty of weed seeds ready to oblige.

I like to get the soil ready to plant, but then not plant it. A few days later we rake or harrow the field and remove a whole flush of infant weedlings. You can see the tiny white strands of their roots and shoots even before they emerge. Now we sow the vegetable seeds.

If it doesn't rain, three days later we are raking and harrowing right over rows we've just planted. The deeper vegetable seeds aren't harmed by the scratching overhead, but millions of those invisible, infant weed seeds are taken care of.

As soon as the vegetables pop up, we pop into the garden with the pointy hoes. The Warren hoe is a triangle with a slightly curved beak, also called an onion hoe. It's perfect for this first weeding, when the crop is so tiny. Sometimes we use a rake and just pull the soil (with its pesky, invisible, infant weedlings) away from the row. We'll pull it back toward the row the next time we hoe it, as our plants will be a bit bigger. A curved garden fork is handy for breaking up the crust around young plants.

As soon as I can see the row, I run the cultivator through the garden and loosen it all up, killing many more of the persistent, pesky, invisible, infant weedlings. I'd rather do this right after hoeing, then not walk on the soil. Each footstep effectively plants the compacted area underneath with a new crop of weed seeds by firming the soil around them so they can sprout.

A rain also sprouts new weed seeds. As soon as it dries up after a shower, we repeat the whole process. Taller plants can have the soil pulled up around their base, which smothers the weeds there. Onions, beets and carrots require more care because they love to have their shoulders exposed.

I continue to get as close to the row as possible with the Farmall 140, sacrificing a few vegetables in order to cut back on the handwork. We have about 200 rows, each about 300 feet long. The first few cultivations are by far the most important. If rain threatens, I often choose to hoe and cultivate a young crop, rather than sow more seed. Keeping it clean is better than growing more. If rain continues for weeks, I'd rather have seed in hand than sprouting amongst those obnoxious, persistent, pesky, invisible infant weedlings.

Here's good advice worth heeding to keep weeds from impeding vegetables you are seeding: before you spy a seedling know the garden is needing thorough raking and weeding.

May 8th, 2007

Hoeing

There has been a lot of hoeing going on around here. Ten miles of rows have been planted, and the inevitable weeds are sprouting along with the crops. It is important to loosen up the earth next to the emerging seedlings so they can breathe.

Short chipping motions cut the soil up and a quick pull though the chipped soil shatters the small clumps. I like it a little moist so the penetration is easier, but it can't be wet because it will form clods rather than break apart.

We want our crop to be able to send their roots wherever they want to go. That's why I love to plow deeply by sticking the shanks in as far as I can get them. The chisel plow can till a foot deep but does not invert the soil like a moldboard plow does. This keeps the subsoil down where it belongs, but opens it up for the roots to get in.

Hoeing is just a tickling of the soil surface, like a light massage. The first time through we pull the dirt away from the little plants. We have to get all the green out; the small grass really wants to cover the newly-bared earth. Nature abhors a vacuum and tries to hide her nakedness with a green dress. We will give her one, but it will be one of our own choice.

Crops like beets grow thickly in the row and we can only hoe the sides. But most of the crops like a bit of elbow room, so we stroke the hoe between them in the row. Leaving the soil surface uneven is helpful, because the hoe goes in easier than if it's perfectly flat. The undulations create more movement, as gravity rolls the dirt, so more weeds get disturbed. The tiny hills and valleys also allow more soil surface to have access to the air.

Air is composed of nitrogen, oxygen and a small percentage of carbon dioxide and water vapor. Plants turn these into carbohydrates and protein. We want the crops to have all the air they need. So after every rain, which seals and flattens the soil surface, we roughen it up again.

I try to keep my back straight and shift my weight around, using both sides of my body. Alternating long and short strokes releases tension which can build up. A little stretching, looking at the sky, and sitting down with the plants breaks up the monotony of being a hoeing machine.

Stepping on hoed ground defeats the purpose. Every step plants weeds because it firms the soil, so then the weeds sprout, and also compacts it, hindering the air flow. Not walking in the garden is a hard lesson to learn. The word "garden" implies a place to walk, but that would be on a path in a more formal flower garden. Our gardens are actually cropland and once they are hoed and fluffed up, we stay off. We're usually pretty tired by then anyway.

When I look down a 300-foot long row, I let the far end pull me through. If there are 20 rows and I have one helper, I'll say, "Let's do this in five hours", which means we'll spend thirty minutes on each row. We need to zip through at about 10 feet per minute. This may only get 80% of the weeds out, but by the end of our five hours we'll be through the whole field. The crop as a whole does better than if we do 100% of the weeding but only get half-way through it. A rain tomorrow, other chores, distractions and unforeseen events may keep us out of the fields for a week or two. If none of this happens, we'll go through it tomorrow and get the other 20% of the weeds out.

This 80/20 rule guides my work. Thank goodness I'm not a perfectionist. Because of the temporal nature of gardening, in a few months the bushhog and plow will wipe the canvas clean, and new seeds will be planted to paint a new picture. In my life, 20% of the weeds are ignored, 20% of the blueberries are left unpicked, 20% of the grass is unmown, and 20% of my life is a mess. But my cup is 80% full.

June 8th, 2010

Laying the Garden By

"Laying the garden by" means doing the final work until harvest, which could be mulching, hilling, or just the last cultivation. There's a point where I know the crop will take over the field, smothering the weed competition. Increasing the biological activity in the soil makes this easier, because of what goes on invisibly in the earth. Tiny, live beings in a rich, humus soil dictate when weeds will sprout or not.

An underground intelligence results from applying large quantities of organic matter in the garden. Traditionally, 50 to 75 tons of composted stable manure gets spread per acre every year on market gardens. Leaf mold, old hay, crop residues and kitchen scraps are also incorporated into the compost and soil. The more diversity of materials the better because we want as many various species of microbes as possible to be present. Herbs wrapped in animal organs have proven especially effective as additions to the composting process. Cover crops, like buckwheat, are invaluable for the good they do, too.

Visitors notice our soils don't bake or crust over, and that they feel silky to the touch. The crumbly texture holds moisture during a drought, but dries out quickly after a downpour. Organic matter offers a buffer against weather extremes, and we're careful to leave the soil loose and fluffy around the young plants.

It's the thousands of different species of underground life forms that make the soil what I call intelligent or sensitive. They remain dormant until needed. They wake up when their particular food source is present. What do they eat? Microbes live on root exudates, the stuff that sloughs off of roots as they grow. They insure their specific food source thrives.

In the squash patch, it's all about the squash-loving microbes. They protect and help feed the squash roots. We encourage them by ridding the patch of all other plant species, so it's just squash roots for them. By the last cultivation, the garden is laid by and they have created conditions in the soil that prevent weeds from sprouting. More cultivation at this point would be detrimental for both the crop we see and their invisible helpers underground.

We lay the corn, beans, potatoes, and peppers with hillers, two rotating discs, which mound the soil up around the stalks. In a smaller garden we'd use a wide hoe to pull the soil towards the plant. Hilling smothers weeds, conserves moisture, and also physically supports the stalks. Most importantly, the soil needs to be loose and friable. Big clods just won't do the trick.

Sweet potatoes, on the other hand, are planted on hilled-up ridges, which then fall apart as I cultivate. We hoe between the plants, and the loose soil falls back in the furrow. When the vines start to sprawl the field is laid by, and their microbes tell the soil "this is sweet potato land for a while."

There are always opportunists, like the pigweeds which the hoe has missed. They stick their vertical stalks above the horizontal vines and head for the sun. When I pull one up, millions of pigweed-loving microbes die and become food for my crop. But if the pigweeds start growing, they send a signal to the soil intelligence that says "this is a good place for pigweeds," and all the pigweed seeds in the soil start to sprout. They also appear when the crop we've laid by has finished growing.

Many of our garden crops are laid by with mulch. We use old hay, as our farm produces a lot of rolls. Tomatoes, cucumbers and summer squashes get mulched just before they start to vine. Again, there are no roots allowed under the mulch except for our crop, and the soil intelligence responds with microbial crop protection, weed suppression, and plant nourishment.

The summer solstice marks a dramatic shift in the forces working on the garden. It's harder to lay a spring crop by, with the sun staying longer in the sky every day and telling everything to grow, grow, grow. After the summer solstice, things calm down a bit. As the sunlight hours decrease, plants become more interested in reproduction and ripening their fruits.

Once the garden is laid by doesn't mean we don't visit it. The enthusiastic passion of the gardener coaxes the pure passionless growth of their plants. Our presence is like a prayer. The tender-loving care we give to the live beings in the earth, and the respect we show to the invisible forces at work in the garden, allow nature to provide us with everything we need.

July 17th, 2007

Moon Signs

Old timers often planted by the moon signs. I'm frequently asked if I do, and I don't know what to say. Although I pay attention to the moon's phases and signs, I generally go about my business regardless of it. The moon obviously affects the water of the earth, and consequently it can't help but affect plant growth.

"However, Nature is not so cruel as to punish man forthwith for his slight inattention and discourtesy to the Moon in sowing and in reaping. We have the full moon twelve times a year, and that is adequate for a sufficiency of the full- moon influences, i.e. of the forces that quicken the fruiting process. If on any occasion we perform what tends to fertilization, not on the full Moon but at the new, it will simply wait in the Earth till the next full Moon. So it gets over our human errors and takes its cue from great Nature." (Agriculture, Rudolf Steiner)

The sun and moon rise in the east and set in the west. They always occupy the same section of the sky; you'll never see them in the north. From our latitude, the sun and moon live in the southern sky between 30° and 72° above the southern horizon. All of the visible planets live in this part of the sky, too. When the sun and the moon block one another, it's called an eclipse. So they call this part of the sky the ecliptic. Twelve constellations are also visible in the ecliptic (at night). Most of them are depicted as animals, so they're called the zodiac, which means "circle of animals." At any given time the sun, moon and the planets are each in front of one or another of these 12 constellations.

For example, on January 6, 2009, the sun is in front of the constellation Sagittarius and the moon is in front of Pisces. We have Mercury in Capricorn and Saturn in Leo. So on this night, January 6, 2009, you'll see Mercury and Jupiter just above the setting sun and Venus is higher in the sky. Saturn won't rise until midnight and Mars is too close to the sun to be visible.

Each of the 12 zodiac signs also represent a part of the human body, with Aries, the head, down to Pisces, the feet. Some of the signs are called barren: Aries, Gemini, Leo, Sagittarius and Aquarius. Some are called fruitful: Taurus, Cancer, Scorpio, Capricorn and Pisces. Two are considered neutral, Virgo and Libra. Farmers and gardeners who "plant by the signs" are referring to which sign the moon is in. January 6th is a good day to plant because the moon is in Pisces. But the sun rules. We have to wait until spring comes. Cancer and Scorpio are regarded as being the two best signs for planting.

When the moon is in Taurus, Gemini, Cancer, Leo, Virgo or Libra it is called a descending moon. This is when the sap runs downward and is a good time for planting and fertilizing. Taurus is high in the sky, and Libra is low. As the moon moves from Scorpio back to Aries, it is an ascending moon and the sap runs upward. This is when we cut brush, harvest crops and prune fruit trees. The moon takes a month to go through the zodiac, just as the sun takes a year.

Another more apparent change in the sky is the monthly cycle of moon phases. Above-ground crops are planted as the moon goes from new moon to full moon, and root crops are planted from full to new moon periods. Our potatoes keep better when harvested during the darker moon phases.

I like to look at constellations. It's hard to believe anything so far away could affect us here. Sometimes I plant by the signs, but I trust that if I plant at the wrong time my seeds will wait until the right sign comes along. Mother Nature knows a lot more about planting times than I do.

January 6th, 2009

Pruning

Hope springs eternal in a young orchard, with untold possibilities in its uncertain future. Branches unfold from the young trunks, later to support seductive apples and climbing children who may not even be born yet. Fifty apples, pears, and cherries make up our home orchard, where grass and deer are not allowed.

Grass and trees are common enemies in the plant world. Trees shade out grass and become deep, dark forests. Grass forms a thick thatch and even exudes a tree-stunting poison, so young fruit trees don't thrive with grass around them. As our little orchard has an 8-foot fence for deer protection, it's also a safe place to grow garden vegetables in between the small trees, and they appreciate the extra compost and loving attention the garden requires.

The annual growth of a tree, sprouting out from last year's limbs, can be compared to annual plants growing in a garden or a meadow. A tree is like a slender hill of earth upon which the new shoots appear. The cambium, a bright green layer directly underneath the bark, connects the foliage with the soil, sort of like a long, skinny root.

I'm pruning the fruit trees so I can throw a Frisbee through them. Any scaffold branch, whose diameter is greater than one third of the trunk where it's attached, may get cut off. If it turns upward and challenges the leader, the central trunk, I prune it.

These two simple principles guide my job and help me make crucial, life-changing decisions quickly. I don't make heading cuts; if the branch needs cutting back, it usually just needs removing. I'm looking for a well-balanced, cone-shape with a strong central leader.

Between 3 and 4 feet from ground level I leave three or four branches whose diameter is less than one third the size of the trunk there. The next tier of scaffold branches is about 2 feet up from the first branches. My shears are sharp, and the cuts are close but not flush, so the branch collar is left on the tree.

Along the scaffold, any upward or downward branches are removed. We want laterals, with nice crotch angles. I try to picture how they'll grow out and eventually shape the tree.

I have ulterior motives in the orchard today, and it's not a game of Frisbee. I'm collecting scion wood for grafting new trees, and in the process observing the growth patterns of the different varieties. For many years, I've offered to make new trees for local folk from old trees on their farms. If you bring me twig from last year's growth this week, I'd be happy to graft it for you.

March 15th, 2005

Orchard

It was a dream come true. After years of fantasizing about a new orchard up on the hilltop overlooking the Long Hungry Creek valley, and many changes of plans, we finally set the trees in the ground yesterday afternoon. A gentle rain, the first in a month, was barely noticeable in my excitement, but when darkness found us planting the last tree, it also found us soaked to the bone.

I've been grafting and planting apple trees since I was a teenager, and our experimental orchard shed light on many lessons for growing fruit. The first lesson I learned was that there is a reason why we don't have commercial apple orchards in Macon County. Early frosts often get the blooms, moist mornings encourage disease, drought is not uncommon, and insect pressure can be intense.

A surprising lesson I had to learn was a little critter called a vole. Looking like a mouse and living underground in mole tunnels, voles love to eat apple tree roots. I inadvertently encouraged them with two things I did. By filling the tree hole back up with rich soil, compost, and leaf mold, I gave them a home. By planting dwarf trees, I gave them their favorite food. Little wonder that in a few years a finely shaped apple tree could be lifted out of the ground with nary a root on it.

Other lessons involved were the differences in about 70 varieties of apples. I looked for disease resistance, productivity, ease of pruning, and the flavor and size of the fruit. I came out of the experience, and the feedback from many people I've sold apple trees to, with a few ideas and a few superb apple varieties.

One simple fruit lesson was to grow pears instead because they are much easier to produce without spraying. In 1996, I set out 18 pears on this hilltop, and we harvested a small peck of them this summer. Magness is my favorite, with Warren and Maxine following closely. They are resistant to fireblight and make delicious pears. I decided there was room for 15 more on the hilltop.

An obvious but hidden lesson about apples is the size of the fruit. If the plum curculio, my worst apple pest, scars a small apple, there is not much left. But on a big apple, you can just eat around it. Also, I found Tennessee grows great summer apples. Because they ripen faster there is less time for suffering drought, disease, and bug problems.

Only late-blooming varieties interest me, as a tree that blooms during an early warm spell often gets its flowers killed by a spring frost. The higher up the orchard is, the farther you are from where the cold air settles, and a slight wind can save those pretty blossoms, too. With the land rolling off three sides, I felt I had a good chance up on this hill. Another way to put this axiom is "a fruit tree loves a good view".

As in most agriculture, soil preparation is the key to success. I filled the manure spreader up several times with biodynamic compost and flung it over the site. Next, I criss-crossed the field with a subsoiler, digging in 2 feet deep on the second pass through each trench to ensure good drainage and to break up the hard pan. Then we spread 400 pounds of granite meal and plowed the land with the spading machine.

I spread lime on the freshly worked soil and sowed a mixture of orchard grass with white, red and crimson clovers, along with wheat as the nurse crop. A harrow was then used to cover the seed.

The biggest chore was the fence. My last orchard, planted in the early 80's, grew at the same time as our deer population did, and they love to eat apple trees. So I knew I had to keep them out, which means an 8 foot tall fence. My neighbor donated cedar posts from a barn project he had abandoned.

Charles let me borrow the auger, and we were soon tamping the posts into the ground along the perimeter of the new orchard site.

It took a long time for me to decide exactly where this permanent, giant fence would go, where to make the gaps, and where the access road would be.

When I heard rain was coming I got motivated. Twelve apple trees were chosen from our little nursery. Mollies for the great size and flavor, the Little Yates for its tasty late apples and good pollinating abilities, the old-fashioned Summer Pearmain and Arkansas Black, and two new varieties I've had good luck with, Fuji and Liberty. My favorite local apple is the Strawberry Apple from Coin Hire in Haysville, and I topped it off with an apple from near the lumber mill that I grafted for Lloyd.

They were all grafted last spring onto standard root stocks, and were carefully dug and loaded into the truck, along with six more buckets of granite meal, two shovels, a digging fork, a big iron bar, some stakes and a hammer.

Up on the hilltop, I lined up the stakes with the existing pear trees, which were six big paces (about 20 feet) apart. It took two people to keep me in line. I set the apple tree stakes eight paces uphill from the pears, as apple trees get bigger. It's hard to picture the full-size tree when you are planting one-year whips. A sadness overwhelmed me when I realized I wouldn't have room left over for a couple of cherry trees, but it passed quickly as I broadened my perspective and saw other possibilities for the new cherry grove.

We set the auger in and drilled out 18 holes before we had a breakdown. The last nine holes we dug by hand. A few scoops of granite meal were mixed into the bottoms of the holes to amend the subsoil, and topsoil filled back the holes. The stakes were reinserted to keep the line of the trees true.

The trees were then planted right where the stakes were by opening the hole back up with the shovel and spreading the roots out a bit and packing in good topsoil around them. I left the graft about an inch or two above ground level. Much of this was done with a handleless shovel because I broke the wooden part off earlier and the other shovel was busy digging the last few holes.

Darkness fell fast on this overcast autumn afternoon, and took me by surprise. I was feeling confident in my stake placement and willful in my intent. We kept going until all 27 trees were in the ground.

Against the twilight sky, the upper leaves waved like little flags announcing the presence of a new orchard. It's still a dream, with many lessons to learn over the next few years as we tend the young orchard, train the trees by pruning, keep the weeds and grass out, protect them from varmints large and small, and patiently wait while the branches fill the spaces between them. When our 11-year-old asked when we'd get fruit, and I said it could be 10 years. She exclaimed, "I'll be 21!"

We all marveled at how time passes by quickly and the gratitude we owe those who have planted trees and broke new farmland before us. We are living their dream while creating our own.

November 27, 2001

Chapter IV

Adventures Of A Truck Farmer

Let's Plant Potatoes
Preparing For Potatoes
Another Potato Crop
Carrots
Onions
Beans
Squashed
Pumpkins
Turnips
Parsnips
Spinach

Gardeners are not perfectionists;
there is simply too much to do.

Jeff

IV

Adventures Of A Truck Farmer

Let's Plant Potatoes

Earth rocks my world. Listening to the music of my fungal hyphae, I decompose the farmer's song and dance routine. 75 tons of beautiful compost give an acre of sod a shiny black coat. At less than two miles per hour, I slip the plow in and gently flip her over. Not too deep but thoroughly penetrating, so nothing is left unturned. We kiss the grass and clover goodbye and prepare for potatoes, those apples of the earth.

Land grounds me. This compacted field has not been turned in thirty years or more. Like meeting a new person, whose familiar smile encourages, the possibilities of a new garden excite imagination. The sensuous aroma fills the air, while smooth ridges and deep furrows follow the hill's contour. I love to fall-plow sod and leave it for Old Man Winter to freeze and thaw it, making us a nice mellow bed to lay potatoes in.

My soul savors soil. Nothing seems as sacred as loosening tight ground and reinvigorating it with compost. An inherent inner instinct awakens and I am silent. I eat from where I walk and do not want to talk. Three hundred bushels of potatoes appear and disappear here every year, followed by similar yields of other vegetables. The souls who support the farm free me from the market economy, and allow my love of this piece of earth to direct my daily work.

Love is not without hurt, and my sensitivity to land creates a pain when I see abandoned farms. Humans cleared and loved these farms, opening up the land for cattle and the opportunities livestock provide. Earth needs animals, especially ruminants. When animals are present the land flourishes, and when absent, it deteriorates. Returning animals from feedlots back to the farms is of the utmost importance.

The four-stomached mammals can create more fertility than what their own fodder requires. The crops they graze improve soil structure. Ancient cultures survived only when this knowledge was recognized and respected. Vegetarianism arose from the realization of the absolute necessity of keeping cattle. Ancient wise men forbid the eating of meat, so that the cattle, sheep and goats survived the years of famine. Otherwise, famine would have ended their agriculture and their civilization.

What happens to grass during its eighteen days in the belly of a cow? The magic of microbes, of intestinal flora and fauna, transform it into the earth's redemption. We further this process in the compost pile. Forces are lost from the growing of plants and are returned to the earth by microbes. Frequently fermenting the farm's forgotten foul fortunes fosters future field fertility.

Molded by mold, backed by bacteria and pro-protozoa, I sense a microbial intelligence in humus-rich soil. When the earth is soft, fluffy and silky, and I can easily move my hands around in it, and our crops grow effortlessly. Microorganisms colonize the roots, ex changing nutrients, water, and protection for the root exudates they live on. This symbiotic, underground relationship creates permanent soil vitality and the best possible sustenance for man and beast. Nature knows what is best for the earth.

Textbooks written for children a hundred years ago eloquently describe these good farming practices: appropriate animal impact, composting of manures and farm wastes, crop and animal rotations, growing green manure cover crops, and the use of rock dusts. It was not only immoral but also illegal to sell hay off leased land, or to not grow the grass and clover two out of every four years. Land was never left idle like we witness so commonly today.

Centuries of experience culminated in these wisdoms about how to use ruminants to build a live soil humus capable of feeding not only the animals and humans on the farm, but also allowing for the sustainable exportation of excess produce. This excess production is food: carbohydrates, sugars, starches, and protein. These are primarily carbon, hydrogen, oxygen, and nitrogen, given to the farm freely from the air and rain, powered by the sun. All we need is love, and the earth to love. Let's plant potatoes!

November 24th, 2009

Preparing for Potatoes

For 25 consecutive years our farm has grown between a half-acre and an acre of potatoes. It's a good crop for our area so I've tried to learn what I can about them as well as from them. My many mistakes have taught me well, and this year's harvest is a bumper crop, despite a major drought in the middle of the growing season. If Macon County needed a cash crop to replace tobacco, potatoes would be a good candidate.

One mistake is planting too early. We wait until the end of March or beginning of April to plant. This allows the ground to warm up and dry out a bit more. The hard freeze in early April would have hurt the plants had they been up. Potatoes come back after being frosted, but expend energy in the process. Planting later allows for more pre-planting, weed suppressing measures, too.

Learning where potatoes fit into a crop rotation plan has helped immensely. Potatoes like new ground, meaning freshly turned sod. The soil must be crumbly and full of humus or the Colorado potato beetles will invade. Clover is the ideal, and this year's crop followed a two year stand of White Dutch clover that was so pretty I was reluctant to plow it under. Life is change, and the diversity of crops makes for a healthy farm, so goodbye clover.

Manuring is the older term for fertilizing, with good reason. Market gardens require 50 tons per acre per year of well composted cow manure for optimum results, according to old farming books. I generally use 15 to 20 tons instead, and spread 20 tons on the freshly mowed clover field last November. But I had extra this spring, and gave the land another 20 loads. I attribute the luxuriant growth during the May and June drought to this, as compost with the decaying sod formed a sponge-like humus that held moisture, even when none fell.

The only other "manure" I used was colloidal phosphate. It's a naturally mined ore, and our soils lack phosphate. We spread it at the rate of 400 to 500 pounds pre acre, every other year. We don't use lime for potatoes, as they'll get scab if we do, but spread it on the land after harvest.

I've learned to plow slowly and not too deeply. I keep my hand on the lift and raise the plow if I see yellow subsoil turning up. I used an Oliver, two-bottom moldboard plow in November, gently flipping over the clover sod, about 5 inches deep. The freezing and thawing during winter helps to pulverize the soil. Plowing too fast destroys the texture of the ground. We want to retain the nice work our grass and clover have accomplished underground over the last two years.

The dry weather in March allowed me a rare chance to run the subsoiler through the field. This tool simply makes a trench, but it is two feet deep. It cracks the subsoil but does not bring the subsoil to the surface. Rains can now enter farther into the ground instead of running off. With the access of air, biological activity increases to a greater depth, eventually forming a deeper topsoil.

Biodynamic preparations of horn manure and barrel compost were stirred and sprinkled on the land to help humus formation. We do this in both fall and spring. I like to ensure the potato-loving microbes are present when the potatoes start to grow.

In early March I broke the field with the chisel plow, also called a rebreaker. I like to cross plow a week later, and then do a final pass lengthwise with the section harrows chained behind right before planting. I make the rows with the Farmall 140, which is what I subsequently cultivate them with.

The rows are 300 feet long, and there are 37 of them. The spacing is about 45 inches between rows. This allows for comfortable cultivating. Any closer (which some were) means I smash branches from the next row. If the rows are too far apart, a strip of weeds is left. Taking time to lay the rows out is definitely worthwhile. They are about three inches deep.

We've done a lot of work without even touching a potato yet. Pre-planting soil preparation pays off. Beetles and diseases are Mother Nature's way of building humus by destroying plants so they decay and form humus. If the soil is in good heart, she finds no need to send in her helpers. We utilize the nearby pastures, cattle and hay fields to insure our potato land already has plenty of humus.

July 24th, 2007

Another Potato Crop

Unfortunately for me, my dad taught me how to cut up potatoes. Many who grew up in the depression years have a parsimonious nature, so every little eye of the potato was used, to the extent of saving the insides to cook. I now know to plant larger pieces, leaving egg-sized potatoes whole, and we are halving or quartering the others with a good chunk of the potato left to help feed the new start. We like to cut them a few days before planting so they heal over and are less likely to rot, and we are careful not to confuse the stem end for an eye.

Each potato piece is dropped into the furrow, and then stepped on. This firmly tucks it into the earth. We plant them about a foot apart, and try to have the eye pointing upward. The cultivator and harrow cover up the rows. The dates were March 22 and 23, while a new moon was in the earth sign of the bull (the neck). This year we planted 200 pounds of Red Pontiac, 200 of Red LaSoda, 500 Kennebecs and 50 Yukon Golds. A few pounds of the last two varieties were retrieved from storage in the cave to finish out their respective rows. I've experimented with dozens of different varieties, and have found these locally available ones to be the best for here.

Ten days after planting I went over the whole field with the cultivator and harrow again. This kills sprouting weeds but doesn't bother the more deeply planted potatoes. When I saw the first one sprout, I again harrowed the field, trying to keep the soil loose and the weeds from sprouting. If a few potato plants get knocked back, it is still worth all the weeds in the row that die. Once the rows are visible the harrow comes off and I simply cultivate, hugging one side of the row. I then double-plow, meaning I travel the same row back the other direction, hugging the other side. I can get within an inch or two of the potato plant, which quickly jumps up and starts shading out the weeds in the row. I stay on top of cultivating, trying to get in there a few days after any rainfall. I want to keep the soil loose, conserve moisture, and keep weeds from sprouting.

The potatoes grew and then bloomed like crazy. I could not find one potato beetle. I put disc hillers on for the last pass, which mounded up soil around the plants. I was tempted to cultivate one more time, but resisted. I've made the mistake of cultivating when the plants were too mature, destroying weeds but at the expense of destroying the potato roots, too. So I left the patch alone, and everything grew.

By mid-July, in the new moon again, the vines were dead and a three foot tall crop of foxtail and pigweeds covered the field. I took the back wheel off the bushhog and mowed down each row, trying to get as close to the ground as I could without cutting into the soil and chopping up the potatoes. One of my past mistakes was that I left the wheel on, which ran right over the rows, smashing spuds. Rather than using the potato plow, which digs them up nicely but covers them back up with soil, I decided on a new method. I put on the subsoiler, and dug the shoe below the potatoes and used the hydraulic lift to raise them to the surface. By going very slowly and staying right in the row, each hill of potatoes was lifted to the surface.

Now comes the handwork. On hands and knees we crawled up and down each row, digging with our fingers to bring up every potato. We left them in piles along the row to dry out for a few hours, and then roughly sorted and basketed them. It took about an hour and a half to get down a row, and another half an hour to put them in the bushel baskets. Each row made about eight bushels, and three rows filled up the pickup truck, two baskets deep. It is a hot, dirty job with temperatures pushing 100 degrees, and a jump in the pond never felt so good. After a week of this we have about 300 bushels of Macon County's finest in the cave. We'll be sorting them all again, but at least it'll be in the cool of the cave.

What I like about growing potatoes is that there is not much cost in growing a big patch. We have to buy the seed, the phosphate, and fuel for the tractors and trucks. We buy baskets and have many other expenses raising cattle, hay and keeping the farm going. But a guaranteed market, like they had for tobacco, would make potato growing a viable way to make a living on a Macon County farm. There could be a processing plant for chips or fries, or a wholesale distributor to grocery stores. Potatoes, like tobacco, fit in well on a small cattle farm that can produce its own fertility. They have certainly helped our farm, besides teaching me many valuable lessons.

July 31st, 2007

Carrots

Five years ago I produced a TV show about carrots, in which I made a "carrot box". This was for home gardeners who had trouble raising carrots in heavy clay soils. The box was filled with sand, compost and good soil. I took the opportunity to explain rock dusts such as rock phosphate, granite meal and lime. But it's not the way I raise carrots now.

We have four rows of carrots, each almost 300 feet long. The ground gets the usual treatment; well limed and well composted. Carrots like aged compost and need a loose soil that's easy to penetrate. Minerals are important too. The ground rocks from apatite, granite and limestone add valuable phosphate, potassium, calcium respectively, and many trace elements, also. The whole garden gets the same treatment.

"Plant early in spring as soon as the ground can be worked" turns out to be bad advice. Yes, you can plant carrots early because they are very cold hardy. For 30 years I planted carrots in March. Then a few years ago I planted a second crop in late April and they did fine. The March plantings are slow to germinate. Carrots will sprout in cold soil, but it takes two or three weeks. Carrots planted a month later sprout up in one week. Okay, the first planting is still a week or two ahead, and will mature a little quicker. But, and it's a big but, weeds don't have a problem sprouting in the cold soil. As a matter of fact, weeds grow pretty easily. Three weeks in spring turns bare soil into a green carpet of weeds, which makes it hard to find a tiny carrot seedling. One of our main research projects here on the farm is how to cut down on time spent weeding. I'd rather get the ground ready, let the weeds sprout, and then take care of them mechanically. So with carrots, the answer is simply to plant them later. The late April sowing is up in a week, and we immediately rake the soil away from the row, killing the sprouting weeds. But I'm ahead of myself.

Most furrows are made with a narrow bottom, so the seeds are in a thin straight line. With carrots, and beets, I use a wide hoe and make a four or five inch wide bottom in the furrow, which is quite shallow. I sprinkle the carrot seed, shaking my hand so it scatters over the whole furrow. It's okay if it scatters outside the furrow, too. Seed is cheap and I buy it by the pound, so a little waste doesn't bother me. The important thing is to get a good stand of carrots four or five inches wide all the way down the row, ideally about an inch apart. We rake over the row, and as soon as they're up we are in there. Once they get their true leaves, I go over the row with the Farmall. The first hoeings immediately follow, keeping the soil loose so weeds don't even think about sprouting. In a month the carrot tops start helping to shade out the soil next to them, and in two months we're looking like Bugs Bunny.

They are often way too thick. We thin them by pulling bunches from the row, but leaving a few carrots to mature into bigger ones. At first, a 300-foot row yields five bushels of baby carrots, but last week we got our five bushels from a third of a row, because the carrots are bigger. Danvers Half- long is the variety we grow. It's a hardy, big carrot that does well here. We have Scarlet Nantes, too. I've tried many carrot varieties, but they are not all that different. Good soil is where good carrot flavor comes from.

When the TV folks came this spring to film a show on onions, I offered to do one on the beautiful carrot field. Greta said no, we'd already done carrots. She likes shows more for a small home gardener rather than how we grow them in big quantities. So when they re-run the carrot show, realize that's not how I grow my carrots. Don't believe everything you see on TV.

August 5th, 2008

Onions

The onion makes the meal. It's one of the oldest domesticated plants, and the many different varieties of alliums are all easy to grow. Garlic, the strongest member of the onion family, can be seen hanging around the drying shed, while the storage onions cover the floor.

Is an onion a root? Although they grow underground, like carrots and beets, the actual root is below the part we eat. An onion is all leaf. Each leaf becomes a layer of the bulb, reaching and wrapping all the way down to the roots. Like Swiss chard and other leaf crops, onions are heavy feeders and frost hardy. Soil preparation begins in the fall.

Two tons of biodynamic compost were spread on one tenth of an acre of a clover cover crop last October, and then slowly plowed in. Gentle plowing retains soil structure. The ridges are left over the winter to freeze and thaw, which helps pulverize the clods. Two hundred pounds of lime were sprinkled on top, and another ton of compost was spread before the rebreaker and harrow finished preparing the ground in mid-March.

You can either plant sets or seedlings; we use both. Sets are small bulbs grown the year before, usually less than an inch in diameter. We toss them by the handful into a two inch deep furrow and cover them up. If you don't want crooked ones you can plant each one upright, an inch or two apart. The soil is kept loose with cultivation, hoes, and finger work. Weeds are not allowed.

In two months, we are harvesting green onions, but we leave one every four or five inches to mature into a bulb. Yellow Ebenezer is the yellow variety, and White Bermuda the white one. Onions from sets are the easiest to grow, but are not as high quality and storable as those grown from seed. The small black seeds are sown in a cold frame in late September, and slowly the slender seedlings sprout and grow. If we had a greenhouse, we could start them in January. But they overwinter fine and are ready by mid-March. You can buy "bunches" of onion plants, a bunch being 60 to 75 plants. They are set out five or six inches apart and the soil is kept loose. We cultivate before we see any weeds. A stitch in time saves nine. One hour stirring bare soil turns into nine hours after the weeds appear and gain a foothold.

By the end of their third month, the tops of all the onions start dying. I aid this process by bending them over with my feet. A week later they are pulled and left to dry in the field for a day or two, and then gently gathered up and further cured on the floor of an open-air shed. After thoroughly drying, so the skins will rattle, onions can be stored in net sacks or tied up in bunches or braids.

Onion varieties are grouped according to day length. The northern, long day varieties need more daylight hours than we get in the south. Although it doesn't keep well, Walla Walla is a popular Vidalia onion. For storage purposes, Copra can't be beat. It's the one we grow and is day-neutral, it can grow anywhere. Old farmsteads often have walking onions, a top-setting perennial. These and other multiplying onions have been grown beside the kitchens of the world since time immemorial, supplying green leaves and bulbs whenever needed. The bulblets form on top, fall over and then sprout new plants, thus they "walk" around the perennial bed. A small bulb yields a bigger bulb, and you plant a big bulb to get many small bulbs.

The world is an onion, and tears form as we peel back layer upon layer of illusion. Everything from the root up of an onion is edible, health-giving, and delicious. From their hollow leaves that look like stalks, to their underground root-like bulbs, onions are simply all leaf, and a gardener's and chef's delight.

July 16th, 2008

Beans

Air is 78% nitrogen. As a farmer, this makes me happy. Plant growth requires a lot of nitrogen and I don't want to buy it. So we grow beans.

In mid-May I make furrows about two inches deep in a well-composted garden spot. We drop a couple of beans from last year's garden every foot, and then step on them to firm the seed into the earth. Dry soil is raked over the top and in a few days they are up and running.

Beans are in the legume family, which loves calcium. I lime the soil where I want to grow beans. The plants have a symbiotic relationship with a bacteria that allows atmospheric nitrogen to get into the soil. An acre of legumes can breathe in 100 pounds of nitrogen, which is great for the next crop. The seed can be coated with an inoculant to ensure the bacteria is present, or you can put some soil in the row from where you grew beans last year.

"The entire organism of the plant-world is divided into two when we contemplate it in relation to nitrogen. Observe it as a kind of nitrogen-breathing, and the entire organism of the plant-world is thus divided. On the one hand, where we encounter any species of legumes, we are observing as it were the paths of the breathing, and where we find any other plants, there we are looking at the remaining organs, which breathe in a far more hidden way and have indeed other specific functions. We must learn to regard the plant-world in this way. Every plant species must appear to us, placed in the total organism of the plant-world, like the single human organs in the total organism of man." (Agriculture, R. Steiner)

Legumes are the lungs of the earth, breathing in nitrogen from the air. Beans were second only to potatoes in the gardens of yesteryear. They are a great source of protein, vitamins and energy. Not only are they good food, they're good for the soil too, and easy as beans to grow.

Fresh shelly beans are picked when the pods are leathery. The pinto type we grow is Dwarf Horticulture, and they turn a beautiful red with yellow streaks. The plump beans don't need long to cook. If you eat beans you'll fall in love with fresh ones.

The other shelly bean we grow is Black Turtle. These are smaller. I don't get around to harvesting many of the beans when fresh; we let them dry on the vine. Then we pull the plants, pluck off the dry pods, and put them up in the barn loft to continue drying. It's fun to sit on the porch next to a friend and visit while shelling beans.

Beans come true, which means you can save seed easily. But I found an interesting plant that looks like a cross between the pinto and black bean. I've never noticed one before, but it's bigger than the black bean and the pod has the pinto spots, but the seed is a deep purple color. Maybe I'll plant these seeds and see what happens next year.

Beans are an important part of our diet, so we grow many long rows. When I pull up a plant, I can see the small white nodules that have swelled on the roots. This is nitrogen from the air that will fertilize our next crop. Beans, breath and air are food for us, food for the soil, and food for thought.

August 18th, 2009

Squashed

We don't want to sell vegetables, but we grew too much winter squash for the members of our CSA. So I called a few other community supported agriculture farms to see if they needed any, and they did. Some potatoes were asked for, too, and a count in the cave determined we had extra.

Winter squash come in many varieties, and they are easy to grow. After mowing down the winter cover crop of crimson clover in late May, an acre gets 30 tons of compost and a couple of passes with the chisel plow. Rows are laid off and we drop two seeds every foot and step on them.

The reason I plant them so close (about 6") is because the big leaves of the squash plants shade out the other weeds, and then we can easily hoe them out to about 18" apart. Otherwise, if planted 18" apart, the space between would be solid grass and weeds. They are covered up and poke their heads up in a few days. We cultivate while we can, using a "knife" for the last pass. This is a long steel blade that attaches on the outer clamp of the cultivator and points inward, so it cultivates under the vines without disturbing them.

Pruning shears are used to clip the stems off at harvest. The shells are hard and colorful. Dark green acorns have an orange spot where they've laid on the ground. Small Wonder is the spaghetti squash we grow, and there are plenty of Carnivals, Delicatas, and Sweet Dumplings. But the Butternuts are our favorite, keeping well into the following year.

Tony called from Atlanta wondering if I needed any granite meal. I said sure. He needed to get a corn grinder here and I love having the granite for compost making. Granite has potassium and many trace elements that our soils lack, so it is appreciated by our microbes.

A CSA in North Georgia ordered a ton of squash, and the health food store there placed an order, too. It was good timing, and we filled his truck up and kissed that squash goodbye. Two CSAs near Chattanooga placed an order, and also got us an account at the health food store there. Adding it all up, I think I need that big truck again. The Knoxville food co-op always orders from us this time of year. We like their store, and will send them watermelons to go with their squash and potatoes. Membership owned co-ops are the best.

20,000 pounds of squash looks pretty, piled up high in every shed available. Someone said that it must be nice to look at it every day and I replied, "It will look a lot nicer when it's gone." Food ought to be free. Then everyone would have plenty to eat. I don't like selling it. I let the customers price it, as I have no idea what it's worth. Organic produce is hot these days, so I'm always surprised at its value. I'm glad we give so much away.

Boxes are found at the grocery stores here, and we wipe, sort and count out vegetables for several days. Into the van they go, and then down the road. It lightens our farm to be relieved of a few more tons of produce. Our own CSA has no need to worry. They get all of the squash and potatoes they want. Neighbors are welcome to get some, too. Only the excess is shipped out, and only for a few months. I breathe a little easier now that I don't feel so squashed.

September 15th, 2009

Pumpkins

As fall approaches on the farm, we gather in the pumpkins. I've experimented with many varieties, and settled on this one. It's called the Old Time Tennessee Pumpkin. A local family gave me a start many years ago, and when it's fed to livestock they call it the Cow Pumpkin or Hog Pumpkin.

I planted a row next to five rows of Connecticut Field and Howden, your standard orange Jack-o-lantern varieties. Besides being a better keeper and the best for pies, the one row out-yielded the other five. And I like the tan color just fine.

Studying up, I found it to be similar to a variety from Southern France called Musquée de Provence, and it's also quite like the Long Island Cheese Pumpkin. These are both in the Moschata family of cucurbitus, a close relative of butternuts. That explains its qualities of taste, storage and production, as well as the similar color.

If grown near butternuts, you'll get some crossing. Another Moschata variety we grow is an Italian heirloom called Trombocini. It's used as a summer squash when small, and makes a long, skinny shape when mature. We've had a bit of crossing.

We made a mistake/discovery this summer. I asked the interns to pick the crookneck squashes, but they didn't stop there, and picked two bushels of immature butternuts. I sent them to our CSA customers anyway. They loved them and want them again next year.

I sorted out the prettiest pumpkins and set them around my cabin. They keep all winter, and toward the end of May, we split them, scoop out the seeds and sprinkle them six inches apart in rows three-and-a-half-feet wide. After a few cultivations, the vigorous vines take over and that's it until harvest. Five heaping truckloads came off of eight, 300 foot long rows.

The butternut family seems more resistant to insects. Because they root along the vine, they can survive squash borers, which attack the stem. You can hill up around the stem, or wrap it in burlap, to prevent the pretty moth from laying her eggs there.

Don't plant too early, like I have done in years past. Nobody wants pumpkins in August, and they like hot weather anyway. For an orange color, we grow Jack-Be-Little, which make cute displays in the house. Another fun one to grow and save seed from is Cushaw, a large, green variety that does not cross with other squashes. They make good pies and are also decorative.

Autumn begins when the pumpkins come in. Since we farm with no irrigation, old tractors and only compost for fertilizer, I call it old-time farming. So it's natural that I love to grow the Old Time Tennessee Pumpkin.

September 21st, 2010

Turnips

He used to turn up his nose at turnips, but now he knows better. They are easy to grow, good for you and your soil, and come in a variety of shapes and colors. Both the greens and the roots are edible, and livestock enjoy them, too.

Purple Top is the most common variety, and can get quite large. Seven Tops are grown mostly for the greens. We are trying two new kinds this year. Scarlet Queen is a fire engine red with tall, tender greens and a sweet, crisp root. The Japanese white turnip has an extra flavor that the catalog describes as fruity, but I wouldn't go that far.

We don't sow turnip seed until mid-August, and it can be planted until the end of September. Any good garden soil will grow turnips. Often, a freshly dug potato patch offers a good spot to sow turnips in. But whenever you've harvested the last of your beans, squash, cucumbers, or melons, you have a prime spot for turnips.

After tilling the soil, thinly spread the seed over the whole patch. They do not need to be planted in rows, but can simply be broadcast. This is not as easy at it sounds, because the seeds are tiny and it is easy to plant them too thickly. An ounce of seed needs to be spread evenly over a four-foot-wide bed, 100-feet long. I pinch the seeds with my fingers and let them roll off, swinging my arm back and forth across the bed. Sometimes I mix the seed thoroughly with a gallon of sand, and throw handfuls over the field. A light raking or harrowing is sufficient for covering them up. Soon the familiar tulip-shaped cotyledons appear, followed by quick-growing leaves. Weeding is usually unnecessary, although galinsoga overtook one of our turnip patches due to Jack Frost's late appearance.

Harvesting is easy. Just pull them up or cut them off, depending on what you want. We peel the roots and eat them raw. They are tastier with salt, in my opinion. The greens are cooked and served a number of ways. My father loved cooked turnips, and Roy just suggested frying the roots in butter.

For the last few years I've been mixing turnip seed in with our cover crop of crimson clover. It helps nurse the slow growing clover along, and improves the soil with its rank growth and decaying roots. With the way they smell, I assume turnips add sulfur to the soil.

The seed is easy to collect. Over-wintered turnips will send up a stalk with flowers and then pods. We pull or cut them, and let them dry on a tarp. Then we walk on the tarp and gradually bring it all to the center, where the heavier seeds fall to the bottom. By pouring them into a bucket with a slight wind or fan, fairly clean seed will fall straight down while the chaff blows away.

Turnips have been sown and grown for over 2000 years, supplementing humanity's diet of grains and meat. Although not as fancy as their relatives, the radishes and the rutabagas, or kale and cauliflower, they will always have a place in the garden.

November 23rd, 2004

Parsnips

Winter is like a parsnip, fit for feeding livestock and not much else. Both are white and long, with deep treasures buried in the earth. I bet winter would be good sliced and baked with olive oil and rosemary, though I've only tried parsnips this way. Parsnips, and winters, too, need a little dressing up to be enjoyable.

Gardeners have been growing parsnips since before the time of Christ, whose birthday marks the beginning of winter. They are planted around Easter and stay in the ground longer than any other vegetable, because it is the freezing temperatures which sweeten them up.

As a member of the umbelliferae family of plants, they are slow to germinate. We plant them shallowly in mid-April in rows 18 inches apart. When their grass-like cotyledons poke up, we hoe the beds. We keep out the weeds until the foliage gets tall enough to shade the soil. Then we mulch the bed with old hay and leave them until late fall.

Their cousins, carrots, have become much more popular with gardeners. Carrots grow quicker, they are sweeter, more tender, and much more orange. But parsnips still hold a place in a few hearts and gardens. Their main attribute is ease of storage, we just leave them in the ground all winter long and can dig up a fresh garden vegetable anytime until spring.

Our 100-year-old cookbook, the one extolling parsnips' virtues as stock feed and little else, does offer a few recipes. They are mashed after boiling, made into patties with an egg and flour, and then fried in lard for parsnip fritters. Stir- frying in butter after boiling and slicing the parsnips turns them golden and sweet. Any meat dish can have parsnips baked along with the potatoes and carrots.

Winter's long nights offer space and time for reading and catching up on studies and hobbies. Inside ourselves are hidden many wonders, tapering the deeper we go. The sweetest things will be found under the darkest shadows.

Last winter's parsnip article brought a sweet couple to our garden. They were from upstate New York, I believe, and hadn't heard of anyone raising parsnips since they'd moved south. We were in the field with several bushels of parsnips dug, and many more to go, when they expressed their fondness for parsnips. We gave them some, and when we heard what they had in mind, we gave them a bushel. Early the next spring, two bottles of parsnip wine appeared on the front porch.

Italians believe pigs raised on parsnips are more flavorful, and medieval doctors prescribed the parsnip for a wide array of ailments, including toothaches, stomachaches, and impotence. I think parsnips are like winter, they need a hot fire, enough fat, and a little time to stew.

December 14th, 2004

Spinach

Spinach loves cool weather, so growing it in Tennessee can be tricky. It certainly tricked me, but eventually I caught on.

In the Midwest, we always planted spinach in spring, as soon as the ground can be worked. But that didn't work here. Even an early March planting of spinach suffers from those hot April days, which make it want to bolt. Give warmth to spinach and up goes the flower and seed stalk. The season for eating spring-planted spinach is way too short.

So we plant in late October or early November. The short cool days sprout it, but that's about all. After narrow, grass- like seed leaves appear, it gets a few true leaves and then remains dormant through the cold part of winter.

I broadcast a pound of spinach seed over two beds, each four foot wide. One was 300 feet long, and in late December we covered it with Reemay, a plant bed cloth. The other bed was about half as long and did not get covered. By early March we were picking leaves. This winter wasn't super cold, and the uncovered bed did fine. It's great to be harvesting it at the time I used to be planting it.

A good, humus-rich soil will easily grow spinach. A slight bit of weeding and soil loosening after winter helps it along. I don't get too crazy though, as it won't last long and will be turned under for a May crop of beans or squash.

Bloomsdale Long Standing is the standard variety, and the one I like best. With the traditional, dark green, savoyed leaves, it lends itself to many recipes. The French likened spinach to virgin beeswax, because its unassuming flavor is impressionable and doesn't overwhelm the dish it is used in. We find it a delicious alternative to kale, which we love but has been our only green through most of the winter.

Oxalic acid is found in spinach, and also in chard and beet greens. It's not good to eat too much of it. Even fall-planted spinach has a short season, so I don't worry about overeating it. Spinach is generally regarded as being healthy for you, just ask Popeye.

I like spinach in omelets and raw in salads. It doesn't take long to cook. I rinse it three times (the low lying leaves get dirty), and then cook it quickly in the water that's left on them. Two or three minutes are all it needs to wilt down. I also like it sautéed with garlic.

We are probably at the southern limit of where spinach grows. March is perfect for it. That is, perfect for growing it. Get it planted in the fall and overwinter it, so by March it is already established and ready to produce. April's warm weather will put an end to spinach, but provide a beginning to many more great things to come.

April 17th, 2008

Chapter V

A Garden Needs A Farm

Farm Chores
Hay
Cattle
Electric Fence
Wood Ashes
Granite
Phosphate
Cedar
Setting Posts
Stretching Wire
Inside Our Skin

A garden grows best from out of a farm.

Jeff

V

A Garden Needs A Farm

Farm Chores

To provide enough vegetables for a few hundred families, I have to get out of the gardens frequently for farm chores. Fixing fences, moving cattle, and making hay are integral work in vegetable production here. Throughout history, wealth has been measured in manure, as a pile of silver won't grow food.

Growing grass heals the earth, building up the soil's humus by thatch formation and decay. When a cow grazes, or I mow, a portion of the roots die with the removal of the leaves. Rotting roots structure the soil by leaving a network of air pockets through the clay, stimulating life as only air can do. Fescue, although not the most nutritious grass, is a master at soil building and erosion control, and has turned worn-out farmland in a positive direction since its widespread introduction during the Great Depression.

Further encouragement for soil life comes from the other end of the grazing cows. The very word manure means fertilizer, and has long been recognized as essential for continued farm production. Thoughts like these compensate for barbed wire cuts, chasing runaway calves, and the many bouncy hours of mowing, raking and moving the hay crop. I never seem to have adequate fences, but I do have perceptive cattle willing to show me where the inadequacies are.

Another essential ingredient for food production on our farm is the native hardwood forest which divides the 100 acres of grass into dozens of small meadows. Following the springs and branches like fractal fingers, the lengthy interface of the woods and pastures create an edge which provides a rich haven for a diversity of beneficial flora and fauna. It's also a slap in the face for the farmer's first round on the tractor, with shrubbery and low branches reaching out for the sunshine and finding my nose instead.

The peace of our garden hides the battles of life and death raging around the farm. Trees competing with grassland, insects and animals eating each other and the plants, and underground microscopic wars are being waged by bacteria, fungi, protozoa and nematodes. The more life there is, the more death follows, and the more that's left over to grow the crops.

One week and 98 rolls later, the fall hay is in. Back in the garden we use a little to mulch the fall greens. It was nice to brush up against the farm's periphery, but the garden feels more like home. Cultivation brings comfort.

October 3rd, 2006

Hay

A garden needs a farm, so last week I shifted focus a bit and cut hay. We make hay while the sun shines, but it gets rained on sometimes. It's an important crop for a variety of reasons.

Our land used to be forest, and supported wildlife and Native Americans. After the invasion, much of the forest was cleared to grow crops. Serious soil erosion followed. Our weather and soils are different than in Europe, and hard rains washed the soil into the rivers. Forest soils erode quickly when planted in corn. Great conservation measures were enacted during the 1930's, and farmers were encouraged to plant hilly land in fescue. Fescue isn't a high protein feed by any means, but it held the soil. Eventually, it built soil. When it is cut, some of the roots die back and form humus.

Clover is the companion plant for grass. Its deep tap root occupies a different layer of soil than the shallow, thatch forming fescue. As a legume, clover can add nitrogen to the soil. We help it by never spreading nitrogen fertilizer on the hay, as this kills the nitrogen-fixing bacteria which live on the legume roots, resulting in soil compaction, the yellow- flowered buttercup weed, and the need to add more nitrogen every year.

Hay becomes feed for cattle, who also help build soil. A farm with an appropriate amount of livestock increases its fertility through proper management. This excess fertility creates the possibility for gardens. Hay and manure make excellent compost.

Around and around the fields we go. Turkey nests and baby fawns remind us of the way Native Americans "farmed". They simply ringed unproductive forest trees, leaving oak, chestnut, beech, and other trees that made food for their "livestock". Indians didn't need fences, either.

After a few days, and a few thundershowers, it's back on the tractor to rake. Around and around we go again. You'd think we'd get dizzy. Sun and wind offer their assistance, and the hay cures out. Soon big rolls dot the green fields. The shaggy-looking farm now looks manicured. By cutting hay and feeding cattle, we ensure good gardens. This is why people like to mow lawns. The fresh cut grass reminds us instinctually that soils are being well taken care of and food production is possible.

I am back on the tractor one more time to get the rolls out of the field and stored away until winter. The nearby grazing cattle seem unconcerned. They are busy eating, and don't seem worried about food for next winter. A tail goes up and the magic fertilizer is spread.

The gardens survived a few days of my negligence. The weeds look happy, but they won't be for long. Once we take care of them, our crops will take over and enjoy the cow-powered soil all to themselves. Some old hay will find its way on directly as a mulch. The rest will have to wait to be digested, spend 18 days in the magic cow tummy, and then be composted for a year before it gets to the garden to help grow our food.

June 12th, 2008

Cattle

The domestication of cattle and the dawn of civilization go hand in hand. One could not have happened without the other. It's easy to see that animals could only be tamed and tended by groups of people who were settling down and forming civil societies. The word "cattle" comes from words that meant "goods" or "money", indicating that animals were the first form of wealth and exchange. Trade is one of the beginnings of civilization, and cattle were right there.

It's harder for people now to accept the idea that civilization needs cattle. After all, vegetarians live quite well without animals, and the raising of animals causes untold pollution, erosion and waste. And, we are told, red meat is bad for your cholesterol levels and your health.

I was a vegetarian for ten years while raising beef cattle and many of my friends are still vegetarians. How did the principals of vegetarianism arise? Ancient wise men realized the necessity of cattle for civilization, and the religious leaders put a ban on eating them for this reason. If a famine came and people ate all the livestock, their society would collapse. The groups of people who evolved vegetarianism love cattle, live with them and worship them.

Why? A ruminant's (cattle, sheep, goats) unique digestive system provides the answer. These animals can live on marginal land, maintaining its fertility, and provide excess fertility for other crops. For example, a 1,100 pound cow needs two acres for its feed, but can supply enough fertilizer for four acres.

When cattle are properly managed, there is very little pollution, erosion or waste. We are properly appalled by modern feedlot-style factory farming. A cow is not meant to eat grain, but grass. The grain is grown with fertilizers, herbicides and pesticides which hurt the land, upsetting the delicate balance in the soil ecosystem. Humus becomes depleted when no manure is returned to the soil. On the other hand, the excess manure in a feedlot becomes a big waste problem. Getting cattle dispersed throughout the farmland and not concentrated in feedlots is the ultimate goal of the organic farming movement.

When cattle are grass-fed on pasture alone, they grow more slowly and live longer. I've had cows reach 25 years old. Recent research indicates the cholesterol and health problems associated with red meat only apply to feedlot cattle. The meat from cattle that are not fed grains does not raise cholesterol levels and is not bad for you.

We're feeding out hay now, and making compost from the wastes. I can't imagine trying to run a farm without cattle. Who would eat the hillside grass? Where would we get humus from? What would we fertilize with?

I respect vegetarianism, and am repulsed by modern feedlot practices. But don't get the wrong idea about cows, they are wonderful animals. (Don't quote me on this when all of mine are out on Heady Ridge Road.) I don't think civilization could survive on this planet without cattle. We are that interconnected, whether we eat them or not. When farms don't have cattle, humus levels drop and it is necessary to bring in fertilizers and other inputs to maintain production. I grew up in the Midwest just as the cattle were leaving the farms, and witnessed firsthand the deterioration of the soil, the rivers, and eventually the community. Farms got bigger, used more chemicals, and were eventually bought up by large corporations. The vibrant rural villages are now ghost towns. Civilization depends on the wise use of cattle, and the way we treat them is reflected in our own health and the social health of our communities.

January 15th, 2008

Electric Fence

I long resisted using electric fencing, but currently see the potential it has to generate a positive influence on our ground. The negative conduct of the cattle forced me to switch over from barbed wire. So, we plugged in poles and a circuit and it shocked me how well it regulated them and now my interest is sparked.

Old perimeter fences of rusty wire are not holding up to bovine pressure. Over the last few years we've experimented with more frequent pasture rotation, and the cattle love it... too much. Now they decide when to move to a new meadow, not bothering to wait for me. The electric fence puts an end to that, it quickly earns their respect.

The posts are set about 10 or 12 paces apart. A corner of the pond is included for a watering hole. To feed, I unplug the charger, drop a few posts, and then bring in a few rolls of the nearby hay.

We strung two different kinds of wire, the old-fashioned steel wire and the newer nylon wire with thin aluminum strands. The nylon one is easier to roll back up but loses the juice if the strands break. Two times we circled the field, to have a low wire for the calves and a higher wire for the cows.

Roaming, roving herds of ruminants are responsible for creating the best soils in the world. By grazing the grass down, the roots die back and make a thatch, eventually forming humus. Their manure and urine add valuable fertility to the land, and their hooves tromping around sort of till the surface and force new seeds to sprout.

The key to this being a good thing is that they are always on the move. If cattle stay in one place for long, the grass gets overgrazed, there is too much excrement for the soil's healthy digestion, and they pack the soil and tear it up a lot.

In the wild, the movers of grazing animals are the carnivorous predators. Whether it's a pack of lions chasing gazelles, wolf packs following deer, or Indians hunting buffalo, the results are equally beneficial for the soil. A large herd of animals mows the herbage, fertilizes and roughs up an area, and then gets chased off. The land rests for a few months with no animals on it, forming humus and growing back stronger than ever.

Large herbivores can destroy the land if they aren't moved off it to get the needed rest. Once we remove the predators, it's up to us to manage the cattle. The best plan is to mimic nature's way. To have a herd in a small place for a small time works best. Then they are moved on and not brought back until the land and grass have recovered and it needs grazing again. This new growth is the most nutritious for the animals.

Electric fence is highly movable, and is the easiest way to get started with intensive grazing and pasture rotation. 30 head of cattle can be on this acre today, that one tomorrow, and around the farm in 40 or 50 days, which allows the first paddock to grow back and be ready for them again. Electric is the buzz word, but don't touch that wire.

February 20th, 2007

Wood Ashes

Wood ashes make a valuable contribution to the soil. A tree's root goes deep into the earth to pull up the nutrients it needs. Many years of growing have left minerals in the wood. These are not destroyed by fire, but are still in the ash.

The word "potash" reveals its origin, the results of combustion, and it is the root of the name given to the element potassium. Plants require potassium, and wood ashes contain about 4 to 5% potassium.

Calcium is the other macronutrient in wood ashes. Both calcium and potassium are cations, positively charged ions. This means they are alkaline and raise the soil pH. They're good for acid soils, which ours tend to be. Calcium is also found in limestone, as calcium carbonate.

Ashes are caustic, and it's not good for you to get them on your skin. Lye soap is made from wood ash. Because of its caustic nature, ash is not mixed with manure, as its chemical action drives the ammonia from the manure into the air.

Trace elements are also found in wood ashes. These are nutrients that plants need in small amounts. I imagine different species of trees have various amounts of the different trace elements. Only dry ashes are valuable, as rain leaches out the nutrients. I clean out the wood stove into an ash bucket and wait until the coals are cold, which can be a few days.

One gallon of wood ashes covers about 1000-square feet of garden. The ash bucket looks like it holds about two gallons, and I fling it 10-feet on either side of me as I walk about 100-feet through the garden. I sprinkle it on as if I was putting black pepper on my eggs. I spread lime on about five times thicker, as if it were salt on my eggs.

Don't put it on too thick, it can alter your pH too much (and don't put ash and lime on your eggs).

We've been burning brush piles, and then spreading the ash on our fields. The black charcoal is also valuable, but for a different reason. It is carbon, the unburned residue, and has lots of air spaces in it. When incorporated into the soil, these air spaces become safe havens and homes for soil microbes. Recent archeological excavations in South America indicate that pre-Columbian civilizations made charcoal, mixed with finished compost, to use for reinvigorating the microbiology of the soil. We can learn a lot by studying how ancient peoples kept their land fertile. Wood ashes and charcoal were, and still are, important soil amendments, and easy to make from your own farm.

January 27th, 2009

Granite

Granite rock occurs in several North American mountain ranges, including the Appalachians, the Rockies, and the Sierra Nevada. It's an igneous rock formed by the slow cooling and crystallization of molten magma. Organic gardeners value the sand left over from granite mines as a natural source of potassium and trace elements. I brought back a truckload from Atlanta last weekend.

Macon County doesn't have granite, and our soils need to be remineralized. I love spreading rock dusts on the farmland and mixing it into the compost piles. Earthworms use granite dust as grit in their digestive process, making it more available as plant food when it returns to the soil. Granite's sparkle indicates the presence of quartz, which is silica. It's in the feldspar family. Ours came from a huge outcropping of granite near Stone Mountain, Georgia.

Potassium is the K in NPK, and our crops need it. It makes for healthy stalks and roots in the plant. Researchers in Connecticut during the 1940's found granite dust to be a valuable fertilizer for tobacco, a crop that needs liberal amounts of potash. They used two tons per acre and produced high yields with no other potassium fertilizer.

The percent of potash in granite sand varies. It can be from 3% to 8%, with 5% being the generally recognized average. The fineness determines how readily available it will be. Some of the small stones I spread probably won't be used as plant food in my lifetime. Adding rock dusts to compost piles enlivens them. When microbes utilize minerals, and then die, the minerals have gone through a live being. Plants are then more able to use them. Fungal activity can release unavailable minerals by colonizing a plant root and the rock at the same time.

One of the problems with water soluble artificial fertilizers, like potassium sulfate, is the detrimental effects they have on these fungi. Sulfur, although a necessary plant nutrient itself, is a fungicide and destroys the beneficial potassium-fixing organisms. Then, even though the soil may have plenty of potassium, it's locked up and unavailable. So, you have to put more water soluble fertilizer on each year. (This is not a problem for those who sell fertilizer)

Another problem is the imbalance of nutrients when we follow human intelligence to fertilize our crops. As the sun shines on the leaf, it wilts and the plant must uptake water. When the soil water is flushed with NPK, the plant takes it up whether it needs it or not. The resulting growth of the plant is then unnatural, and nature often sends her humus-building helpers, insects and diseases, to the soil's rescue. (This is not a problem for those who sell pesticides and fungicides.)

In a live soil humus, a microbiological intelligence rules. The soil water is more pure, so when a plant needs water, that's what it gets. If it needs a nutrient, a signal is sent to the microbes. They find it, and make it available to the plant. Because they live on plant root exudates, it is in their best interest to grow a healthy plant, which they know how to do much better than us.

I shoveled about 100 pounds on top of a couple of compost piles. I'll mix it in with a fork. I also spread some on the hay and manure that I'll be making compost with. About 700 pounds were simply broadcast on an acre of garden with both a cover crop and several tons of compost on it. This is called sheet composting. Any way of getting mountain rocks ground up and on the garden helps plants grow better.

January 9th, 2007

Phosphate

Fifty years ago, Dad read an ad. "Buy another farm", it said. "By spreading Tennessee rock phosphate, you will double your farm's yields, so investing in it is like buying a whole new farm." Many of the farmers in Illinois used the phosphate rock from Tennessee with excellent results. When I moved here and became an organic farmer, he told me this story and recommended I look up Robin Jones Phosphate, somewhere south of Nashville.

But by the mid 70's the mine was closed, and all of the rock phosphate came from a lower-quality quarry in Florida. Old farming books say Florida's is 18 – 30% phosphate, while Tennessee's is 30 – 35%. Tennessee Brown Sugar, as it was called, was the farmer's choice for a natural rock phosphate fertilizer. Only a small part, 2 or 3%, of this phosphate is readily available, the rest is slowly released for many years. It's a long-term investment.

Most farmers now use superphosphate, which is the rock phosphate treated with sulfuric acid or phosphoric acid to make the phosphorus more readily available (i.e. water soluble). A problem with this is that a large percent leaches into the water in the runoff. Phosphorus is a pollutant in rivers in the Midwest farm country.

Phosphorus is a major plant nutrient, the P in NPK. It helps plants ripen their fruits, increases root development, improves the quality of the crop, and helps plants to resist disease. Bone meal is an excellent source of phosphorus, which leads to an interesting observation because manure lacks it. So the animal as a whole can supply all of our fertilizer only if the bones find their way back to the soil.

Manure-based organic farming operations, like ours, need to add phosphorus to their fields, so we add rock phosphate, which is a lot cheaper than bone meal. Rock phosphate contains other nutrients essential for plant growth, such as boron, zinc, nickel and iodine. These are lost when it is treated to make superphosphate. Also, the sulfur in superphosphate causes an imbalance in the microbiological population in the soil because the bacteria which multiply in sulfur's presence destroy beneficial soil fungi, particularly the phosphate-fixing microbes which help make the unavailable form of it available to plants. Other nutrients that rock phosphate have are calcium, iron, copper, magnesium and silica.

Imagine my delight to find Tennessee rock phosphate is available once again. My farm, like many others, is deficient in phosphorus, and I knew if I could remedy this we could get better stands of clover and our crops would benefit as well. I had one-and-a-half truckloads hauled up from Columbia, Tennessee, and then the fun began.

I rented a three-point hitch fertilizer slinger which was minuscule next to my 34-ton pile. So my next plan was to ask at the farm supply store to borrow a fertilizer spreader, but I had never used one. He told me it may not work because the phosphate was so dense, and he was right. But diligent poking with a hoe handle every so often kept the stuff from packing, and we slowly started getting it spread.

We found the spreader worked best if we only put one front end loader bucketful in it. It also worked better if we hauled the phosphate to the field with the bucket and then put it in the spreader because driving with the spreader full tended to pack the dirt-like material.

I was aiming for a rate of 400 – 500 pounds per acre, and wanted to cover 100 acres with 25 tons. The gardens, orchards, and cropland got a double dose, 1,000 pounds of it, and if I drove a half of a mile, I'd be covering about 2 acres with each load.

It required a lot of stopping and poking with a hoe to keep it flowing. The bumps in our fields, which make haying a hassle, actually helped keep the phosphate flowing by jarring it a little. Gradually the pile shrunk and our farm's fields got a light brown dusting of the long-awaited phosphate fix. Charles's garden will get a shot of phosphate for the generous contribution of his front-end loader.

We filled feed sacks and stashed them in the barn. This we will spread on the fall gardens which are still full of cabbages and other greens. I scraped up the last of it, mixed with a little soil, to be used in our composting. Rock phosphate is very beneficial in compost because it helps hold some of the nitrogen and adds the nutrients which manure lacks, so the compost is richer and better balanced as a fertilizer.

Three days later, we are spreading the last load as night falls and a rainstorm moves in. The soil soaks up the phosphate, and I'm thankful to get it on just in the nick of time, before the fields are too wet to drive on. I can't wait to see the difference it makes in next year's crops. I've always wanted Tennessee phosphate ever since my Dad told me about how well it worked on his farm.

Phosphorus means "the light-bearer". It is often the most needed fertilizer and there are not unlimited supplies of it. We are lucky to have such a good quality source of it here in our own state. So, if you want a new farm, sprinkle your present one with some Tennessee Brown Sugar and your crops will dance and taste so good.

December 11th, 2001

Cedar

Cedar trees abound in Tennessee, providing farms with an invaluable resource – fence posts. A farm needs cattle, cattle require fencing, and cedar's rot-resistant wood supplies the posts. We dropped several last week and set 39 posts in, but this fence is not just for cows. It's to keep the deer out. In the early '70s, a rare sight of deer prancing across the field added a beautiful animal touch to the serene, green landscape. They have since become a major agricultural pest, but the revenue deer hunting brings to our state probably exceeds farming. To successfully practice horticulture you have to keep the deer out.

An acre atop the hill needed a deer fence so we could grow sweet potatoes, beans, squash, peppers and watermelons. The other fenced garden has long been growing them, and our ability to rotate crops became limited. The deer demolished our butternut crop last season, and that was the last straw.

When a field is no longer farmed, cedars are among the first succession of trees to sprout up among the weeds and briars. Our farm has reforestation efforts in many stages, with cedars inevitably leading the way. Some of our hillsides were abandoned long before I arrived, and the full grown cedars, with just a bit of foliage at the top, are being over-shadowed now by the secondary forest growth of oak, hickory, beech and maple. These older, declining cedars have the most red in them, and make the best fence posts.

Dropping a tall cedar among taller trees can prove difficult. Several factors need to be taken into consideration. We look to see which way it's leaning or has the most weight, where other trees might be in the way, how we're going to snake it out, and what I'll do if it starts falling the wrong way. A deep-notch cut into the side we'd like it to go is made first. A path is cleared to get out of the way if it falls differently, and the cut on the back brings it down.

Sometimes we had to hook a chain and tractor up and give the hung up tree a tug. Next we trimmed off the branches, and cedars have plenty of them. I like to place the longer branches perpendicular to the hillside so they collect leaves and create small contours that help check erosion. Soon a bunch of 12-foot long logs surrounded the knoll.

A simple rectangle around an acre would have the fence going up and down the slope too much. It took a while, and lots of walking, to finally decide exactly where this fence would be. It turned out to be a heptagon - a seven-sided fence roughly following the contour around the hilltop. Plastic electric fence posts were set (and moved a hundred times) at 12 paces apart, with an extra post 8 feet from the corners and gateways, for the bracing. I had to be sure this immovable construction project was in the right place.

Three 16-foot entrances are included, two facing the different roads, and one near the future composting site. The hay from the adjacent field is lined up inside the fence next to the garden. I'll take it out to a nearby flat spot to feed the cows and eventually make compost piles, which will be returned to the garden a year later. Thus, the surrounding pasture will sustainably keep the garden fertile.

Some of the logs would have made lumber, but we are farmers, not woodworkers. So we took the sledge and wedge to a few, splitting them in half. The distinctive aroma and pretty, pinkish-red hues rewarded our efforts. The biggest logs left became the corner posts, and the rest were dragged to their respective future homes, marked with the plastic posts.

Utilizing farm resources such as these cedars for protecting farm crops appeals to me more than the idea of just selling them. Cedars are beautiful habitats for birds. The small, blue berries are used to flavor gin. Although cedars are host to a devastating disease of certain apple varieties (the cedar- apple rust which makes orange spots on the fruits and leaves of apple trees), their value to the farm as a whole outweighs my lack of Yellow Delicious apples. Besides, unless they're grown inside a fence, the deer will eat the apple trees anyway.

January 16th, 2007

Setting Posts

I like the number 39, but 40 is easier to say, and it sounds better when describing how many posts we set. An auger helped get us going, but I kept shearing the 7/16" bolts off. A safety guard must be removed and replaced each time, and after a dozen times I got pretty good at it. Not happy, just good.

The big iron bar broke through the rocks and eventually the holes were shoveled clean to at least two feet deep. We chainsawed off the white part of the cedars, as only the red part contains the oils which keep them from rotting. The white will decay as quickly as any wood, but the red will last for decades.

Down by the creekside we filled buckets with fist-sized stones. After lining the posts up, we began the laborious job of tamping rocks into the holes around the posts. First, a little clay, then pounding in a few pounds of stones, then more clay, then more pounding. The post gradually got tighter. Backing off, we eyeballed it and shifted it if necessary to get it perfectly vertical. A few required a gentle shove or pull with the tractor, as we got them tight too soon.

After a few days, all of the posts were set in place. The next step was bracing. Seven corners and three entrances meant 14 braces. Along with a few smaller trees, the tops supplied most of our brace posts.

First, I squared off the fat end and flattened the top near it. Then Phil held it at an angle and I cut a notch in the bottom of the post we'd set 8 feet from the corner. I whittled both the post and brace until they fit, if you can call using a chainsaw "whittling".

The next step was to cut the brace a little longer than it needed to be, and flatten the bottom where it went in the notch. Then we cut the notch in the corner post at head height and tried to get the brace to fit, which involved more whittling. A barn pole nail then got hammered through the brace into the bottom notch.

A horizontal brace was then notched into the two posts at about 6-feet off the ground, near where the top notch was. Flattened ends are made in the brace, and a hammer and chisel help finish the notches in the posts. Before it's nailed we took it down and nailed the top of the angled brace in. Soon we had a braced corner post with a right triangle at its base and a 6-foot high horizontal brace nailed in with 8- inch long nails.

You'd think we'd have gotten better at this as we went along, but our first one was about as good as the others. After a few I get sloppy, not better. Some just work out right, and others don't. A few got cut too short, but luckily were long enough for somewhere else.

Eventually all the braces were up, but we were not quite ready to stretch wire. A chainsaw needed to be run up and down the outer edge of the posts and bracing, so that the wire didn't get hung on the little branch stubs.

Noah had 40 days of rain, and Jesus had 40 days of fasting. I may say we have 40 posts in, but that is one more than the truth. My Uncle Frank never got older than 39, he just kept having his 39th birthday every year. Stretching the truth is easier than stretching a fence.

January 23rd, 2007

Stretching Wire

We've been creating a lot of tension this week. It starts with nailing the end of a roll of wire onto a corner post. 2-inch, barbed steeples are driven next to a vertical strand in at least five different places. The wire is lifted 4 inches off the ground, so we can swing a machete underneath it to keep briars and trees cut back. Two other deer fences were placed flush to the ground and have roses, blackberries, sycamores and elms wanting to grow up and needing to be dug out, so this time we left room to get underneath with something sharp.

An iron bar is woven through the woven wire and chained to the boom and tractor. Slowly I inch forward, and quickly the wire mashes together. Oh yeah, we forget the spacer. A cedar post gets notched and placed between the chains, which are allowed to slide through the boom's hole.

Now we get her tight and nail her up. The next piece is nailed, and then taken back down when it turns out to be too short. A miscalculation worries me. Will we have long enough sections? By midday the 4-foot tall wire is up all around the fence. Once.

It'll take another round to finish, to get it up to 8-feet tall. Climbing the ladder, the end is nailed. Hooking up and pulling slowly, the bar falls out. Or the spacer shifts or the wire breaks. Each time I lower the boom and we start again.

Running out of nails, I start conserving. Only two steeples per post quickens the pace. By dark we have two sections left to do, each about 120-feet long, with two pieces of wire, each about 120-feet long.

Luckily we quit. The next day I realized one section was a little longer, and one piece was a little shorter. I paced it a few times and then we swapped the pieces. Sure enough the long one barely reached, and so did the short one. We stretched 2000-feet of woven wire and have less than 20- feet left over. Too close for comfort, but I'm comfortable now.

More steeples the next day, and we still want to cut off, tuck in, and wrap up our loose ends. I'm not nailing wire to the braces this time. When I inevitably back the tractor into the post, it'll be easier to fix. I'm speaking from experience here.

The gates will be simple wire gaps for the time being. Someday (over the rainbow), I'm going to have nice swinging gates on all of my fences. It'll be a dream to open up a latch and let her swing, rather than untying two ropes and dragging the post and wire back and forth.

Our cover crop is sighing in relief, free to grow with no deer to graze it down. Beans, sweet potatoes, you name it, and now we can grow it. It's a high-tension fence, but I'll be a lot less tense not having the deer eating the garden.

February 6th, 2007

Inside Our Skin

Picturing the farm as a living organism, the property line would be the skin. What happens inside is largely determined by me, the farmer, and what happens outside the skin is mostly beyond my control. It's nice to have a buffer of woods and hedgerows along the edges.

In order to export 100,000 pounds of produce from the farm to Nashville each year, a certain amount of activity has to take place within the border. Like instruments in an orchestra, the diverse parts must play together in harmony. The conductor, the farmer, ensures that everyone plays their part, but the music comes from higher places.

The magnificent, Eastern hardwood forest is one of the most marvelous phenomena in the world. Home to a larger diversity of plants and animals than many locales, we get lots of help from them for our crops. From the birds and the bees to the mammals and the trees, life is continually birthing and decaying in the woods. This activity is of immense benefit to the land, from the tiny microbes to the giant white oaks.

That doesn't mean we should never cut down a tree. If a tree's diameter at breast height is 2-feet or more, it could be carefully removed to let younger trees fill in the space. Logging is only done in winter, when the sap is down, so that valuable nutrients are left in the woodland soil. We've never cut hardwoods, because I'd like our woods to become an example of an old growth forest.

The hardwood trees eventually shade the cedar trees out, so we select ones without much green on top that don't have much of a future. Actually, their future is a fence to keep the deer out of a hilltop field where I'd like to practice horticulture. The forest is donating to the garden for the export of vegetables.

Twenty years ago I quit mowing some steep land going down to a small creek. Because of the great strength of our special forestland, we don't have to plant trees. Cedars sprouted up and now underneath them come the poplars and other hardwoods. The farm organism lives not only in this space, but also in time. Many years from now there will be more fence posts, followed by a hardwood forest.

The pastures and cattle are the digestive organs, creating enough extra fertility to grow all the produce. Building a live humus soil buffers the farm from excessive moisture or drought conditions. By encouraging insects and fungi we keep the small percentage of damaging ones from disrupting things.

Creeks and springs circulate water through the farm. By opening up the soil and not logging, the rain that falls soaks into the ground. We'll need it later next summer.

At the heart of the farm are the humans, directing what goes on. Only through the interaction of the people and the land is wealth created from nothing. The more we do within our borders, the healthier our farm is. This health allows us to send excess carbon, oxygen, hydrogen, and nitrogen, (in the form of carbohydrates, starches, sugars and proteins), gained freely from air and water, to those outside our skin who support this vibrant, living organism. Our thanks go out to all who allow us to work on the farm.

December 28th, 2010

Chapter VI

What Is Biodynamics?

Biodynamics
Peasant Wit
Silica
Yarrow
Chamomile
Stinging Nettle
White Oak Bark
Dandelion
Valerian
Applying The Compost Preparations
BD Ditty

To see the bigger picture,
it helps to occasionally close your eyes.

Jeff

VI

What Is Biodynamics?

Biodynamics

What is the difference between organic and biodynamic?

Both are farming methods which contrast drastically with the chemical agriculture so common today. They both attempt to build up the soil's humus content, and rely on biological activity for fertility and pest control. The use of toxic chemicals - whether insecticides, herbicides, fungicides, or fertilizers - is strictly forbidden. Their differences are not as numerous as their similarities.

Everything we do on our biodynamic farm allows us to be certified organic, but the reverse is not true. Biodynamics has stricter rules on what can be used, and also has further requirements that organics doesn't. The restrictions are in regards to soil fertility, pest control, and cultural techniques. The requirements are the use of homeopathic preparations made from herbs and animal organs.

How a farm maintains soil fertility is at the heart of the agricultural question. A biodynamic farm is ideally self-contained, having the proper amount of land with livestock on it, so that excess fertility is available for other crops. All the feed for the animals is grown on the farm. The only inputs allowed are ground rock powders such as limestone, granite meal, or rock phosphate to help remineralize the soil. Compost is made from materials found on the farm. As a remedy to help rebuild worn-out farmland, a limited amount of a neighbor's cattle manure can be allowed, provided it's free of chemicals and composted before it's used.

Organic farms also use manure and compost, but it doesn't have to be generated from the farm. They do not have to raise livestock like a biodynamic farm does. The manure can come from commercial animal operations such as chicken factory farms, large scale confinement feed lots, or modern dairy farms. These places use practices that biodynamics doesn't support.

An organic farm can use fish emulsion, cottonseed meal, potassium sulfate, calcium nitrate, and other fertilizers in limited amounts. The fish are of unknown origin, cotton is highly sprayed, and water soluble fertilizers hurt soil microorganisms, so we don't use these fertilizers. But they are better than what commercial agriculture uses.

For insect control, organics permit insecticides such as Rotenone, Pyrethrin, soaps, oils, and other non-synthetic bug deterrents. Again, these are certainly less toxic than what else is available, but biodynamic farming simply doesn't deal with bugs directly. We rely on a humus-rich soil growing healthy plants which don't attract excess insect damage.

Plastic, for mulch, is not used much on a biodynamic farm, although we have grown strawberries on it. We have no greenhouse and don't irrigate. We grow in-season produce and use the water nature provides. Organic farms often use plastic mulch and irrigation, and plastic hoop houses are common. I just don't like plastic.

Food, like wine, has a sense or taste of the place where it's grown when the soil is full of humus. Traditionally, farmers relied on the manure from their animals to keep their fields fertile. Biodynamics, introduced in 1924, articulates the need to use compost and manure from within the farm itself. The organic movement sprung forward with the writings of Albert Howard, Robert Rodale and others, who also spoke out against chemical agriculture, and emphasized the need to use composted manure to rebuild the soil humus.

After the recent rise in demand for organic food, a new type of organic farming appeared, one that relied on off-farm inputs. It is disheartening to see the desire for organic food drive the industry to lower its standards. When the goal of a farm is to be self-sustaining instead of just to make money, agriculture becomes healthier. In biodynamics, what a farm can export must be generated from within the farm itself. This seems to be the main difference between modern organic agriculture and the original model of biodynamics.

April 24th, 2008

Peasant Wit

A farm needs cattle, Dad informed us. It was 1974, and we'd just settled into our Tennessee homestead, which had obviously revolved around livestock. Dad had experienced the deterioration of the soil and the local rural economy in the Midwest during the previous decades, and attributed this to the removal of livestock from cropland.

Nitrogen from cow manure or clover is not the same as nitrogen from a bag. Cattle and the crops they graze can improve the soil's humus content, and manure is the best fertilizer (except for the proverbial farmer's own footsteps). So we got a herd and spent the next 35 years chasing them back into the pastures. They were trying to teach me rotational grazing. The cattle stayed even though we became vegetarians and didn't make much money on them. But the composts we made from our own cows were noticeably superior to what I made from the neighbor's cows. It seemed to break down more quickly and more completely. We wanted to grow all our own food, so we needed cows.

The young farmers received more fatherly wisdom: Don't buy anything. Find or grow what you need on the farm. This was easy to follow given our income level. I was immediately endeared to Rudolf Steiner's Agriculture course when I recognized similar advice.

"Whatever you need for agricultural production, you should try to possess it within the farm itself (including in the "farm", needless to say, the due amount of cattle). A thoroughly healthy farm should be able to produce within itself all that it needs." (Agriculture, R. Steiner)

It is distressing to see a garden with a yellowish hue, denoting a lack of nitrogen, or an abandoned, ungrazed pasture begging for manure. Nitrogen has to be available for plants to grow, but luckily it's everywhere. Air is 78% nitrogen; it is in every breath you take. Steiner has a lot to say about nitrogen. "Nitrogen not only becomes alive but sensitive inside the Earth; and this is of the greatest importance for agriculture. Nitrogen is not unconscious of that which comes from the stars and works itself out in the life of plants, in the life of Earth. Nitrogen is verily the bearer of sensation. So you can penetrate into the intimate life of Nature if you can see the nitrogen everywhere, moving about like flowing, fluctuating feelings."

In organic farming, we want our nitrogen alive, which is why we keep livestock, make compost and grow legumes. Being aware of the nitrogen flow is a large part of the art of agriculture, and apparently it has something to teach us. What can we learn from nitrogen, and how?

"If you knock against a table, you will only be conscious of your own pain. If, however, you rub against it gently, you will be conscious of the surface of the table. So it is when you meditate. By and by you grow into a conscious living experience of the nitrogen all around you. It is not at all a bad thing if he who has farming to do can meditate. He thereby makes himself receptive to the revelations of nitrogen. All kinds of secrets that prevail in farm and farmyard-we suddenly begin to know them."

As we read the Agriculture course, we are continually encouraged to imagine, feel, concentrate and look around us. In his other works, Steiner gives meditation practices using imaginations, feelings, concentrations and observations. We retain in ourselves a little more carbon dioxide in meditating and breathing deeply. It's not easy to just be aware of my breath; all sorts of ideas pop up in my head. I like to look at a seed and picture the plant, or look at an older plant and see the future new plant, or imagine a growing plant and how it is different from a stone, animal or human.

"For when you meditate you live quite differently with the nitrogen which contains the Imaginations. You thereby put yourself in a position which will enable all these things to be effective; you put yourself in this position over against the whole world of plant-growth. For there were times when people knew that by certain definite practices they could make themselves fitted to tend the growth of plants."

The Agriculture course contains certain definite practices. Steiner prefaced the compost preparations by emphasizing that we must provide for oxygen, carbon, hydrogen, nitrogen and sulfur to come together in the right way with other substances, notably with the potash salts. Potash is oxygen and potassium, which is a cation like calcium and magnesium. Yarrow was chosen for its quality of potassium, chamomile for its calcium, and both for their relationship with sulfur.

Plant growth thrives when the cations (positively charged ions) are within this specific ratio: Calcium 64-72%, magnesium 10-12%, and potassium 4-5%. This ratio encourages life in the soil. Rain and air provide much of a plant's requirements for O, C, H, N and S, but we must provide the cations ourselves. We get potassium from wood ashes and granite meal, and calcium and magnesium from lime. The minerals, like the manure, must be present for the magic to happen.

"For there is a hidden alchemy in the organic process. This hidden alchemy really transmutes the potash, for instance, into nitrogen, provided only that the potash is working properly in the organic process. Nay more, it even transforms into nitrogen the limestone, the chalky nature, if it is working rightly. The fact is that under the influence of hydrogen, limestone and potash are constantly being transmuted into something very like nitrogen, and at length into actual nitrogen. And the nitrogen which is formed in this way is of the greatest benefit to plant-growth."

This is the nitrogen I want flowing on our farm - homegrown nitrogen, so to speak. By enclosing the herbs in animal organs and burying them, new and unique humus products are created to add to our compost piles. Alchemy refers not only to the transmutation of elements, but also to the transformations that happen in our souls. The farm offers many opportunities to work on ourselves, along with the other farm chores.

An example is a walk in the woods after being in the garden. The forest air feels thinner and the darkness is disquieting. I'm reminded that the scary scenes in fairy tales often occur deep in the woods. Back in an aromatic meadow my senses calm down, the butterflies act tamer than the birds and the aromas are more earthly. The garden feels the most comfortable to me; it is familiar and homey.

"I do not say clairvoyant, but you can easily become clair-sentient with respect to the sense of smell, especially if you acquire a certain sensitivity to the diverse aromas that proceed from plants growing on the soil, and on the other hand from fruit-tree plantations and from woods and forests. Accustom yourself to specialize your sense of smell; to distinguish, to differentiate, to individualize, as between the scent of earthly plants and the scent of trees. You see, the farmer can easily become clair-sentient."

At another point Steiner asks us to think of a simple peasant-farmer walking over his fields who meditates in the long winter nights. Two ways of looking at the world begin to merge - a scientific one and a romantic one. Without belittling intellectual consciousness or bemoaning the loss of instinctual wisdom, we can develop the latter while retaining the former.

"We go through the fields and all of a sudden the knowledge is there in us. I, in my youth, at least, when I lived among the peasant folk, could witness this again and again. The merely intellectual life is not sufficient; it can never lead into those depths."

Dad was born in 1906, several generations away from intuitive peasant wisdom. Steiner was a bit closer. When we moved to Tennessee, our neighbors still worked horses, lived without electricity, and planted by old proverbs and moon signs. They valued livestock greatly. I could only learn from them by keeping my mind wide open and paying close attention to what they were doing. Steiner was quite the intellectual himself, so I find the comments on his own education enlightening.

"I grew up entirely out of the peasant folk, and in my spirit have always remained there. As I look back on my own life, I must say the most valuable farmer is not the large farmer, but the small peasant farmer who himself as a little boy worked on the farm. In my life this will serve me far more than anything I have subsequently undertaken. I have always considered what the peasants and farmers thought about their things far wiser than what the scientists were thinking."

Helpful, practical advice pours forth from the Agriculture course, and stellar farms worldwide prove its efficacy. Steiner loved both the simple peasant who really knew his or her own farm, and the academic scholar trying to understand the myriad processes occurring on the farm and in Nature. The two views are not mutually exclusive. Farmers and scientists can grow far more together.

"It will always be a beautiful memory to me if this course becomes the starting point for carrying some real and genuine peasant wit into the methods of science."

March 3rd - 17th, 2009
all quotations from Agriculture, R. Steiner

Silica

Nothing helps a clay soil like the addition of sand. Clay has very small particles which hold water well, and it also contains plant nutrients, but it packs and crusts over after a rain. Sand is larger, doesn't pack together, and drains well, but has little fertility. Lime helps loosen a clay soil, too, but as calcium is so water soluble, it leaches out and the soil gets hard again. Sand is not water soluble, so it is a permanent amendment.

When we look at the world as a product of the elemental forces – earth, water, air, and warmth – we associate clay and lime with the first two and sand with the latter two. A sandy soil warms up faster and has more air in it. On the other hand, clay soils are more fertile and moist. Humus ties it all together by bringing in life. All of the microorganisms which build healthy soil are in the organic matter.

Sand is silica, a combination of silicon and oxygen, and it is very prevalent. One-half of the earth's crust is silica. Quartz crystals are silica, and so are computer chips. While lime, compost, cover crops, and other humus-building farming practices strengthen the earth and water forces, adding sand helps the air and warmth forces.

There are sand and quartz crystals everywhere under the ground, and we know little about their importance in agriculture. Not being soluble in water has kept them from being regarded as necessary, but I'd hate to farm without them.

In biodynamic farming, we do an interesting procedure with silica to help plants, not to grow but to ripen and become more nutritious. First, I gather quartz crystals, either from folks who have been to Arkansas digging them, or from local geodes. Crystals are hexagonal, clear, glass-like, and hard, and light sometimes reflects rainbow colors in them.

I love smashing geodes, those spherical, pockmarked rocks found in Macon County streambeds. The insides vary, but are often hollow with beautiful crystal formations. Yesterday, we hammered some up into small chunks and dropped them into an inverted metal fencepost driver. We further crushed them by thrusting in a tamper bar into the cylinder with a good bit of zeal.

We strained the smashed crystals and re-crushed the ones that didn't go through the strainer until we had a quart or so of quartz. To grind it more, I put a tablespoon at a time on a windowpane, and after putting in earplugs, rubbed another pane of glass over it. A loud sh-h-h-h sound turns into a sh-o-o-o sound as the number of particles increases with the grinding. Some of it makes a fine powder, and some is still about the texture of cornmeal.

To this, I add enough water to make a thick paste, and then I stuffed the paste into a cow horn. After filling three horns, we buried them in rich-looking soil in a rock circle above the rock terraces behind the cabin. There they will sit within the earth until fall. When I dig them up, I'll empty the contents into a glass jar which will be stored on a sunny windowsill.

After the garden has grown a bit and the plants are ready to quit growing and start their flowering and fruiting stage, I will reach for the jar of ground quartz. What I've just made won't be ready for this summer's crop, but I have some I've made previously. A half-teaspoonful is dropped in a crock with three gallons of spring water early one morning. As this procedure works with the forces of air, light, and the sun, I like to be at it at the crack of dawn. Now I get to stirring and I vigorously get a swirl going one way until the vortex reaches the bottom of the crock. When I pull my hand out, a mandala forms in the spiraling water, and I evoke chaos by starting to stir in the opposite direction.

An hour of this alternating stirring is sufficient to homeopathically potentize the water with the enhanced crystal forces from the quartz powder we had buried in the cow horn. Potentize means to bring into active force and value the latent power of something. All that is left to do is mist it on the ripening garden to promote nutritional and storage qualities in the produce. Plants treated this way get a nice shine to their skins, which is where the silica in a plant or fruit is, and thus explains why our produce doesn't rot so fast after it's harvested.

Using a preparation like this does not negate the need to add sand to the clay soils, or any of the other good farming practices required to grow high quality produce. But it does allow us to work with the air and light, via the ground crystals, to balance out the earth and water that works with the fertility of the compost and liming materials we've applied.

The horn silica, buried over the summer, is the polarity to the horn manure, which is manure stuffed in a cow horn and buried over the winter. This latter one works with calcium and the forces of growth and reproduction. We stir and sprinkle it in the evening to strengthen the earth and water elements. These two preparations work together harmoniously.

Plant growth lives and weaves in the balance of the earth below and the sun above. I'd be interested to know other ways gardeners use silica to bring a sparkle to their produce and help with the keeping qualities of vegetables and fruits.

April 23rd, 2002

Yarrow

Nature freely supplies much of what a plant needs to grow. Air often contains sulfur, and rain can provide silicic acid, lead, mercury, and arsenic in the minute quantities plants need. On the other hand, we must till and fertilize the soil properly to have the right amounts of phosphate, potash, and limestone. The earth also contains trace elements such as boron, copper, iron and zinc. Plants need all of these things available to them to flourish.

Unlocking and freeing up the earth elements is the job of microbes, and compost is the key. Even if the soil is well fertilized, it is of no use unless the plants have the power to receive the influences the soil contains. Soil bacteria and fungi feed larger microbes, whose life and death releases earth elements they've incorporated into their bodies. Only then can these elements be used by the plants. Microbes are propagated in compost.

Variety is the spice of life, and in the compost pile I say the more the merrier. Small amounts of many different ingredients ensure a greater diversity of microbes, capable of catalyzing various life processes. Living forces are as important for plants as are substances, and we can use specially prepared herbs to impart to the compost a tendency to that living vitality. This will enable the compost to bring the right vitality to the earth itself.

Yarrow helps bring sulfur into a good relationship with potash and the other earth elements in the plant. It is a feathery-leafed, white-flowered plant found in meadows and along the hay fields, and we encourage its growth because of its beneficial microbes. Medicinally, yarrow stops bleeding and is used to treat bladder infections.

In June we take wildflower hikes and gather the umbrella-shaped bouquets in bushel baskets. With scissors, I clip off the tiny white blossoms. I dry a few gallons for later and use the rest by sewing them up in a dried stag's bladder.

What is present in yarrow is intensely preserved by the process which takes place between the kidneys and bladder. We can influence our compost pile with a preparation made by enclosing yarrow in a stag's bladder. A small amount of the resulting humus product enlivens the compost so that the earth can receive what it needs. The bladder gives the yarrow the power to enhance the forces it already possesses, to combine sulfur with the other substances, especially potash.

A buck, with his antenna-like antlers, is a very nervous animal, quite aware of the surrounding environment. When we are nervous, we have to pee. We are sensitive to the outer world through our bladder, but not as much as the buck. The bladder is located at the end of a long tube connecting it to the penis.

A hunter recently brought me a stag bladder. I rehydrated the dried yarrow flowers with a tea made from fresh yarrow leaves. Then I stuffed them into the bladder. I couldn't believe how much it held. The bladder kept stretching and I had to brew more tea and soak more flowers. It must have been a big buck. It held a half gallon of yarrow, and was the size of a softball. I sewed it shut with a needle and thread.

I wrapped it in a piece of nylon screen, to keep the birds off, and hung it in the south eave of the barn. The next one I used held about three pints of yarrow. Now I'm blowing up the other bladders, tying them off, and hanging them to dry. They'll be rehydrated in spring and filled with fresh yarrow flowers. I experiment with different ways of making biodynamic preparations.

After they hang in the sun a while, I bury them about a foot deep in good, humus-rich soil. They are dug up in May, and small amounts are added to all of our compost piles. A year later the compost is spread throughout the gardens, helping our plants get what they need. The biodynamic compost preparations are simple to make, don't cost anything, and create superb compost. They are substances we can use to insure that microbes and life forces are allowing the elements to work together properly, in the compost, the soil, the plants and animals, and eventually in us.

December 8th, 2009

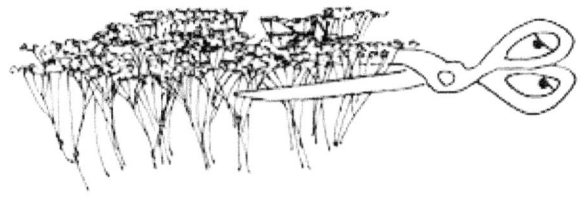

Chamomile

In early summer the delicate flowers of chamomile bloom profusely, creating a pretty, yellow and white carpet over their lacy leaves. We harvest them every few days and lay them on a table in a dark room to dry. Chamomile blossoms aid digestion and are used medicinally for stomach aches and insomnia. They are also one of the flowers buried in an animal organ, and eventually used in our compost piles.

Yarrow, with its unique potassium and sulfur combination, helps give the compost the power to receive so much life into itself that it is able to transmit life to the soil. But we must also make the compost able to bind together the calcium compounds. Chamomile assimilates calcium, along with sulfur, which keeps the plants healthy and free from the harmful effects of fruiting. Calcium is important for moving nitrogen into the plant, and plants need this continual flow during reproduction to remain in good health.

Seeing that chamomile heals our digestion, we want to bury it enclosed in a piece of the intestines. The cow is the supreme example of digestion in the animal world. Unlike the nervous deer sensing every sound and ready to leap away, a cow contentedly chews its cud and allows for human contact. You can hardly find two mammals with more opposite natures.

For eighteen days, grass gradually turns to manure inside the cow. First it goes into a large stomach, the rumen, which looks like a shag carpet inside. There must be miles of surface area, engendering amazing microflora and fauna. Then the cow coughs it back up and chews it again. This time it goes down to the reticulum, and then to the omasum and finally the abomasum.

Each stomach lining is more refined than the one before, and the grass gets to looking more and more like manure. That's what we find in the intestines. This whole process of digestion in ruminants creates the possibility of agriculture, because these animals make more fertilizer than needed for the plants they graze on. The miraculous microbial activity generated inside a cow deserves our awe and respect. The intestines hang on the isles of mesentery, and I cut them off with a sharp knife, being careful not to puncture them. They are a hundred feet long. I rinse them, cut them into foot- long sections, and tie one end off.

Chamomile tea moistens the dried flowers, and a small funnel is inserted into the open end. I stuff the chamomile into the section of intestines and pack it tight. Sometimes I have a blowout where the tie comes off the other end, or a hole opens in the side. But eventually I have a bunch of sausages, with chamomile in them instead of meat.

You may have noticed I did the yarrow two different ways, one with fresh yarrow in a reconstituted, dried stag bladder, and the other with dried flowers, moistened, and sewn up in a fresh bladder. Rudolf Steiner gave the simple instructions for making these compost preparations in 1924, and then died soon after. Biodynamic practitioners ever since have been experimenting because we couldn't get more specific answers to all the questions which arise and the different ways it can be done.

Sometimes I bury the sausages directly, but this time I decided to hang them up like the bladders for a few months. Then I find a place with real rich soil to bury them over the winter. The transformation when I dig them in the spring is obvious. The flowers are gone and a deep brown humus-like substance is inside - slick, shiny, and ready to go into the compost heap.

We get compost with a more stable nitrogen content with the added virtue of kindling the life in the earth. The earth itself will have a wonderfully stimulating effect on the plant growth, creating conditions for truly healthy plants. Chamomile's tiny amount of sulfur attracts calcium compounds and draws them into the organic process. It's the perfect flower to make sausages and to help enliven the compost piles.

December 15th, 2009

Stinging Nettle

A definition of intelligence is the ability to respond successfully to a new situation. This type of intelligence resides in a humus-rich soil which is permeated with beneficial microorganisms. The new situation would be a new crop, and a response is the colonization of the new roots with the specific microbes that create maximum production and crop health.

Some of the plants we use to make the biodynamic preparations might be replaced with something else, but one plant is irreplaceable. Although we like to stroke what we are fond of, we can be very fond of stinging nettle and still not want to stroke it. Small hairs on this plant will make your skin feel likes it is on fire.

Gardeners use tea made from nettle to perk up their plants. Soak one part nettle to ten parts rainwater for a few weeks, stirring it a few times daily, to make a decoction for watering sickly plants. A little peat moss sprinkled on top will keep the odor down.

You wouldn't think it, but stinging nettle makes a delicious pot herb, cooking it like you would spinach. I add it to potato soup. With a high concentration of iron, it is helpful for anemia, and is a great spring tonic. Nettle is especially good for pregnant women and nursing mothers, because it also contains calcium.

With a long-sleeved shirt and gloves, I cut the two-foot long stalks in spring, just as they begin to flower. Then I strip the leaves and blossoms off the stems and pack them tightly into a clay tile. A nylon screen covers both ends of the tile, and it is buried up in the orchard in a pit lined with peat moss. I leave it there for 16 months, so it spends two summers in the earth.

When I dig it up there is not much left. It decomposes into a soft black humus that almost sparkles. I put it into the center of the compost piles in slightly larger amounts than I do the other compost preparations. It can also be added to compost tea. The reason for the clay tile is that when I don't use it I can't find the nettle when I dig it up. It disappears. I think earthworms are the culprits.

This condiment will make the manure intelligent and give it the faculty to make the earth into which the compost is worked intelligent. The soil will individualize itself in a nice relationship to the particular plants which you are growing.

We don't understand all of the microscopic activity involved in plant growth. Although I can rattle off names like enzymes, hormones, auxins, and the various species of bacteria and fungi, I don't know how they help plants grow. It is not so important for me to be intelligent about them. I simply want intelligent soil, and stinging nettle helps.

February 23rd, 2010

White Oak Bark

A large number of plant diseases, although not all, can be prevented by a rational improvement in the way we fertilize our fields. Calcium is important in this regard, as it damps down excess rampant growth, which leads to problems. But ordinary limestone is not sufficient; we need the calcium to be alive to have this healing effect.

The bark of the white oak tree has plenty of calcium, about 77%. Bark represents an intermediate product, between the plant and the living part of the earth. The tree takes up lime from the soil and deposits it in a live form in the bark.

Fertilizing with compost works directly on the earth, rather than filling the soil's water with soluble nutrients. But some does get into the water, and when a plant takes up too much fertilizer the stage is set for other growth to occur on the plant. These varied diseases have trouble gaining a foothold when the plant has access to calcium.

We lime our fields, but it's just ground-up rock. It takes microbes to unlock the calcium. Specific microbes can incorporate calcium from lime into their bodies, and when they die, it is in a form that plants can use. Where do we find these microbes?

One place is in bones. Bone meal is an excellent source of calcium because it was once part of a live animal. The skull of an animal would obviously have the most diverse set of microbes, with all of the sense organs imbedded in it.

Two head from our herd went to the slaughterhouse, and I came back with their heads. I scooped out the brains. Some people eat this, but it has zero appeal for me. I used a long handled spoon, and reached in the hole that goes from the brains to the spine, scooping out the white stuff. Every nerve signal travels through this opening.

In the past I've sprayed water from a hose into the brain cavity, to rinse it out, but this time I decided to leave it unrinsed. My rationale was that any microbes left in there would be beneficial.

I put a cardboard box up against a healthy white oak tree and scraped the bark off with the claw end of a framing hammer. It's silver on the outside and reddish on the inside. I did not dig into the bark; I just took off what came easily. We ground it up in a hand operated, Corona grain mill, and then ran it through a household strainer, regrinding what wouldn't pass through the screen.

The ground oak bark was moistened with warm water to the point where it would hold its shape when I squeezed it. I packed it into the skull, pushing it tightly with a wooden dowel. A tight fitting rock was hammered into the hole to seal it up.

We dug a pit in a marshy spot below where the spring water is always running, and we pulled out a big pile of muck. The skulls were plopped into the water, and the muck was thrown back on top. We finished up by covering the pit with big rocks to keep animals from digging it up. When I remove the skulls, I scoop out the oak bark. It looks darker and has lots of little white bugs crawling around in it. It looks alive. A small amount is added to the compost heaps. A unique, live calcium spreads throughout the pile.

Oak bark changes after spending several months in a skull under water. Our gardens don't have much disease problems. But our tomatoes suffered the same fate as many did during last season's cool, wet July. A disease crept up and wiped them out. I did not get too disheartened, these things happen. I just tried to make a better oak bark preparation this fall and in a few years it will have been in the compost and out in the fields, adding good calcium sources and forces.

January 12th, 2010

Dandelion

Dandelions are one of the first flowers we see blooming on the farm in the springtime, and we're still finding bright yellow blossoms in late December. Early April is when masses of flowers cover the lawn, and that's when we harvest them. A dandelion flower takes three days to mature. On the first day, a few yellow petals surround a button of unopened petals, and that's when we like to pick them. That evening they close back up, and when they open the next morning the button is gone and there are more petals. On the third day, they start looking ragged, and soon form the spherical fluff we can blow away with a wish and a puff.

They're dried in a single layer on a table in the dark, and routinely stirred to prevent molding. Blossoms picked young won't turn to fluff, but need to be thoroughly dried. Dandelions attract silicic acid, which is extremely important for our soils. They have potassium too, and are used medicinally for liver problems, and as a spring tonic. We want to treat the dandelion so that it will give the soil the faculty to attract just as much silicic acid as the plant needs. Then the plant will grow sensitive and draw to itself all that it needs.

Surrounding the stomach of a cow is a yellowish, net-like material called the peritoneum. When I remove it, I mark the inside with a safety pin because I can't tell the inside from the outside once it's free. A tea from dandelion leaves is used to rehydrate the dried flowers. I put the remoistened dandelion blossoms on the inside of a piece of the peritoneum and sew it up like a pillow. I pack them in tightly.

Alternatively, I have used the isles of mesentery. This is a thinner membrane which holds up the intestines. It peels off fairly easily while everything is still warm after butchering. In the agriculture course, Steiner mentions both the mesentery and the peritoneum, and I'm not sure which one he meant.

The dandelion pillows are buried in a good soil in a flowerbed by a sandy spot. They're dug in the spring, and they have definitely rotted into a humus that's black and waxy. They make little balls, and a small amount is added to the compost piles.

Plants do not live in isolation. Everything in nature is in mutual interaction. We can bring about a wonderful interplay in nature by giving the plants the forces which tend to come to them through the dandelion.

These preparations are so simple to make, yet have a profound effect on compost, soils, and crops. Unfortunately, they are not widely known in America like they are in Europe, and in other parts of the world. They are like homeopathic medicines for healing some of the detrimental effects from chemicals and compaction. At very little cost, compost made on the farm, with the addition of these rotted herbs, turns out to be the best way I've found to fertilize and revitalize our soils.

January 19th, 2010

Valerian

I planted a valerian patch yesterday. It felt good to get my hands dirty, cleaning out the chickweed and dead nettle that sprouts up in late winter. I shook the soil off their thick root systems, and loosened the bed deeply with the digging fork.

Sand and compost were then incorporated into the bed. The clay soils that we have benefit from the addition of sand, which helps keep them open. Compost goes on everything around here. A clump of valerian was gently wiggled, and yielded ten individual plants. I tucked them into the flower garden about 18-inches apart. A little water finished the transition to their new home.

The strong smelling roots indicate valerian's medicinal value. "Valeo" is the Latin word meaning strong, an allusion to valerian's medicinal uses and is the root of the name. A strong sedative is made from valerian roots, but that's not what I use it for. I make a medicine with the flowers for the compost heaps and the farm.

Valerian sends up a 4-foot tall stalk with beautiful white flowers tinged with pink. I snip off the florets, and grind them in a mortar and pestle. Next, I add four times their volume of water, and let it ferment a few weeks. Then it's strained and stored in a dark bottle, but I leave the lid a little bit loose at first in case it hasn't finished fermenting.

When I have an abundance of blooms, I make valerian juice. The flowers can be put through a juicer, or ground up in a corona mill and pressed to extract the juice. It has a strong smell and gets stronger after it sits and ferments. The valerian preparation, either way it's made, stores well. All of the compost preparations are carefully tucked into jars with loose-fitting lids (so they can breathe), and placed in wooden boxes full of peat moss. These boxes are inside our root cellar, which does not have electricity running to it.

The horn manure is stored in crocks surrounded by peat moss, and I often make six holes and add a teaspoon each of the compost preparations to it.

There are different ways to add valerian to newly-made compost piles. Yesterday, I simply poured a small amount into a hole. More frequently, I stir a dropperful into a gallon of water for 15 minutes, alternating directions similar to the stirring of horn manure and horn silica preparations. Then, I pour half a gallon into a hole, and sprinkle the whole pile with the other half gallon.

If I add it the first way, without diluting it, I then stir and sprinkle the finished compost pile with valerian right before I spread the compost on the fields. Valerian helps the compost with phosphorous, getting it active to supplement the organic process. Sometimes valerian is stirred and sprayed on fruit blossoms to help ward off a late spring frost, but this did not work when I tried it.

Valerian is a pretty addition to the perennial garden. A dark green rosette overwinters, and the flowers in spring are quite showy. It is one of the characteristic plants in old gardens, prized for its spicy fragrance and proliferation of blooms. Although an old world plant, valerian has a place in today's garden, too.

March 31st, 2010

Applying the Compost Preparations

Section I

An underrated facet of ancient agriculture is the seemingly insignificant amounts of animal bones and organs left over from meals that found their way back into the soil nearby. Recent microbiological discoveries indicate that 75,000 species of bacteria, 36,000 species of fungi, and myriads of protozoa and nematodes play a vital role in soil dynamics. The plant and animal refuse we "throw away" during food preparation are rich in these microbes, whose beneficence for plant growth even in the tiniest amounts can't be denied.

Small amounts of inoculated soil are spread far and wide through the highly-mobile life of larger soil animals. Microbes hitchhike rides with them. Worms, birds, and small mammals continually move them around. Microbes remain dormant until their unique life-support systems are in place, and then they wake up and help. These systems feature plants whose root exudates feed the microbes in exchange for the protection and nutrient extraction the microbes provide.

Modern agricultural methods, with soil compaction and harsh chemicals, can destroy the microbes and their habitat. So we spread compost and rotted manures to reinoculate the soil with beneficial microbes. Along with this, we avoid chemicals and compacting the soil around our crops.

The detrimental effects of chemical agriculture were discernible by the early part of the 20th century. Quality was declining, diseases increasing, and soils were not responsive to this change. The loss of a diverse microbial population led to the need for more and more toxic chemical rescue measures, which, in turn, amplified the problem.

A well-respected scientist and philosopher at the time, Dr. Rudolf Steiner, was approached by farmers observing this rise in animal and plant health problems. He addressed the issue in a lecture course in 1924, published now as the book *Agriculture*. Encouraging every farm to have the proper amount of animals, he also insisted we fertilize with compost and refrain from using artificial fertilizers.

To help revitalize soils, Steiner recommended tiny amounts of specially prepared herbs to be added to manure heaps and compost piles. How were the herbs prepared? By enclosing and decomposing them in animal organs.

Here we have a way of getting the unique microbes in bladders, intestines, skulls and mesenteries back into the soils. Yarrow, chamomile, oak bark and dandelion, all common healing herbs, undergo a transformation in these organs, respectively, and reintroduce the lacking microbes, enzymes, hormones, auxins, and no telling what else. Nettle and valerian are also suggested for the compost, and horsetail as an herbal spray.

It's safe to say we don't understand all of the complex interactions involved in plant growth, but everyone now agrees of the importance of humus. Soil microbes are the master builders and components of humus, and increasing their diversity and numbers can only improve our farmland.

January 3rd, 2006

Section II

Once we've decided to put the biodynamic preparations into our compost piles, we are faced with more decisions. Local biodynamic farmers, like myself, may offer you some, or you can buy a set from Josephine Porter Institute, Box 133, Woolwine, VA 24185. Now you have five teaspoons each of five different rotted herbs and a small vial of a fermented liquid, apparently enough to impart up to fifteen tons of compost or manure with the living forces which will enable it to bring the right vitality into the earth itself.

Repeatedly layering a foot of organic matter like old hay, leaves and garden refuse, with three inches of manure and an inch each of soil and rotten wood chips, will suffice to make good compost. The moisture level needs to be high enough to encourage rotting, but not so much that it excludes air. This amount would be like a damp, but not soaked, sponge. Rock dusts, such as granite meal, greensand, or rock phosphate are also beneficial in the heap, as are kitchen scraps, lawn clippings, and even dead animals. Anything organic will rot and help fertilize your garden.

If the pile is about 12-feet in width, 21-feet long and 6-feet tall, with sloping sides, it is about 15 tons. A concave depression in the top allows rainwater to soak in, often alleviating the need for extra moisture. A "skin" of hay, leaves or rotten wood chips also helps keep the pile moist. A smaller pile still needs a full set of the preparations. I will use more than a teaspoon each if I have plenty, and I add another set when I turn the pile, usually after two months. Then it sits for 8 or 10 months undisturbed.

Twenty years ago I became acquainted with Hugh Lovel, Harvey Lisle and Hugh Courtney. They became my mentors in the use of biodynamic compost preparations. They all noticed a difference in two of them. The nettle and oak bark made their dowsing pendulums swing in the opposite direction from the other four. Consequently, they all recommended placing these two in the center of the pile and the other four around the periphery so that their vortexes don't interfere with each other. I follow this advice, climb up on the pile and make two holes with a stick, about two feet deep and five feet apart. Then I squeeze a handful of soil around a heaping teaspoon of the rotten nettle and push it down into one hole, and fill it back in. I put a rounded teaspoon of the oak bark in the other hole. All of the herbs are put in a ball of soil to ensure that they don't dry out.

At the end of the pile closest to the nettle I make a hole and then make two holes to the left, two holes to the right, and one at the far end. The holes on the left get a teaspoon each of the yarrow and chamomile, and on the right I put a teaspoon of the dandelion in the first hole. The second hole gets a pint of fermented horsetail tea, which is not generally used as a compost preparation, but has been recommended by my mentors for regulating the moisture in the pile. Harvey also likes horn manure in the pile, so I put a heaping teaspoon of it in the first hole at one end of the pile. Next, I stir a teaspoon of the fermented valerian juice in a gallon of water for 15 minutes, alternating vortexes every 20 seconds or so, pour half of it in the hole at the far end of the pile, and sprinkle the other half over the whole pile.

A birds-eye view of this placement of the preparations would show the horn manure, nettle, oak bark and valerian in a line along the length of the pile, with the yarrow and chamomile on the right side, and the dandelion and horsetail on the left side. The dowsing of my teachers confirmed the beneficence of this order, as does my own feelings, intuition, and subsequent observations in the fields over the past 20 years where I've grown crops with the finished compost. I personally do not use dowsing to interpret reality, but I can respect those who do.

January 24th, 2006

Section III

I still interact with my mentors in biodynamics from 20 years ago, and many new folks, too. Hugh Lovel has left his market garden in Georgia and moved to Australia, where he's a farm consultant. He makes reagents from the biodynamic preparations, and places them in jars that are inside a 10-foot long plastic drain pipe that is buried three feet into the ground. A copper plate at the bottom of the pipe is connected by wire to diodes and resonating crystals, and then wrapped around the jars. With dowsing, he confirms that living forces from the preparations radiate out from this field broadcaster and impart vitality to the crops grown nearby.

Harvey Lisle is a retired soil scientist who believes in the power of prayer. He also dowses, and claims the biodynamic preparations, placed in the way I've described, create a high quality compost with yin, or female, energy forces. He balances this with what he calls cosmic compost, which also has yang, or male energy forces. To make cosmic compost, Harvey meditates around his pile, preferably with a friend or two. He asks that the earth, which nourishes us all, pour its forces into the pile, and that the sun and the moon also lend their support and pour forces into the pile. Next, the five visible planets are named and asked to help. The 12 zodiac constellations are then invoked to give their respective forces to the compost pile, and finally the farthest reaches of the universe are called upon to help out, too. He closes the blessing with the names of Jesus Christ and Michael, the guardian spirit of our age.

Hugh Courtney believes that the forces in the preparations need the physical carrier of the preparations to have the full effect in the physical world. A blessing is quite in order, but his direct perception indicates the need to do more than pray or use a field broadcaster. The preparations work under enormously different situations, and how they are placed in the pile is not so critical. The important point is to get them in there. They create a new, live humus in the compost pile, a building-up process that follows the breakdown of the organic matter. You can express your own, and your farm's individuality by the placement, and then check your results by field observations.

During our fall conference, I asked four other farmers to place the preparations in four different compost piles, and I got four new ways to do it. Ruth places nettle in the center, and on each end of a row down the middle of the heap, using three teaspoons to one each of the others. She wanted her pile symmetrical, "like a work of art", covered with a "skin" of hay.

Hugh W. used three sets of preparations to a pile, alternating yarrow and chamomile on one side and nettle and oak bark on the other, with dandelion and valerian on the ends. Lloyd placed one set around the periphery, as recommended by Pfieffer. Luke put a set on one side of the pile, and a second set on the otherside.

This totally fascinates me. I'd love to hear how other folk use the preparations in their piles and on their farms. The practice of biodynamics is unique to each farm and farmer, which has led me to believe that you can't do biodynamics the wrong way. Beginners especially need to know that you can improve your garden and farm immensely with small amounts of these highly-potentized substances, but this is still a new method. Since seven out of the seven successful farmers I asked do it differently, I again claim that you can't do it wrong. There may be better ways, but the important thing is to do it and see what happens.

March 28th, 2006

BD Ditty

With animals and plants
and compost filled with mirth
We partner in the dance
to heal our Mother Earth

Late in June I sing this tune
Tomorrow I'll pick yarrow
I'm making a little bag
From the bladder of a stag
Cutting flowers from the stem
Into the pouch I stuff 'em
Then sewing it tightly up
Under an eave I hang it up
It soaks up the summer sun
In the fall it's still not done
Now it's buried underground
Dug up when spring comes around
A teaspoon for the compost pile
Potassium and sulfur smile

The sweet-scented chamomile
Petals soft and so serene
Heading for the compost pile
With an odd rest in between
The intestines from a cow
Are rinsed and cut up and tied
Pretty flowers are stuffed in now
For sausages who will hide
In humus soil 'til next spring
Then put in the compost pile

Nature spirits dance and sing
Calcium and sulfur smile

You'd best not meddle
With stinging nettle
You will need a glove
For this plant we love
Losing sting with heat
for good greens to eat
Buried in peat moss
Hope it doesn't get lost
Add it to the compost pile
Silica and iron smile

An open-grown white oak tree
Is round just like a wheel
The outer bark is pried free
And ground into a meal
We can find another sphere
Inside a dead cow's head
We scoop out the brains from here
and fill with bark instead
Buried in a swampy spot
Used in compost piling
Disease will bother us not
Calcium is smiling

In the early spring with so much to do
I stop everything to go pick a few
Dandelions
I'm down on my knees in early hours
Before honey bees land on the flowers

Dandelions
I am hunting through the cool morning dew
For the buttons who will tell me they're new
Dandelions
With mesentery I sew a pillow
To hold and carry a bag of yellow
Dandelions
Buried underground until the next May
If they're never found that is where they'll stay
Dandelions
Potash and silica smile
with dandelions in the pile

For the final preparation we use
No animal organ or carrion
We simply gather and press out the juice
From the flowers of the valerian
Ferment it first and stirring it we must
Then sprinkle it over the compost pile
The light-bearing spirit of phosphorus
Joins all the others with a great big smile

Elemental elations
With simple preparations
Heavenly celebrations
Of new humus creations

September 25th, 2007

Chapter VII

We Can Grow All Our Own Food

Sleeping and Waking
I Can
Buddhism
Christianity
Bell's Bend
Extension Agent
Farm Festival
S.S.A.
We Can
Compost Blues

We would all eat much better
and treat the earth like we ought
if food was simply given
and could not be sold or bought.

Jeff

VII

We Can Grow All Our Own Food

Sleeping and Waking

Just as we wake and sleep in our daily rhythm, so does the earth in her annual cycle. A common conception is that the earth wakes in spring, is most alive in summer and then falls back asleep for a winter's rest. In biodynamics, drawing a line at ground level, we take a different view.

The teeming life observable in the lush summertime will be stored in seed and roots underground during winter. The life of the soil is especially strong in winter, the season when the earth is most inwardly alive, and it tends to die down in the summer. I also feel more aware and alive in the cooler months than I do when it's warm outside.

Spring has flown by with summer on her heels, and we've been running non stop ourselves. Between hoeing and haying, picking produce for selling or the cellar, and all the fresh tasks which pop up unannounced like scenes in a dream, there is no time to think. Repetitious farm work can become second nature, not requiring conscious thinking, with the feeling that I'm just another organ in the farm organism.

Taking a break, I stroll by the head-high cosmos with my head in a dream. I remember being wide awake last January, ordering these Bright Lights seeds. The garden is a dream, a dream come true, as the heavenly taste of the first raspberries confirm. My walk reveals more organs of the farm's body: clover meadows and oak forests, flashing springs and a tadpole mudhole, and the flight patterns of June bugs weaving an invisible tapestry over the basil and zinnias. The buckwheat has intense insectual activity, and the flitting swallowtails wonder where the carrots have gone.

In this flying, midsummer's dream, I move by a swimming hole full of kids, themselves full of raw, sweet corn. They are dreaming of watermelons ("how long till they're ripe?"), and the next pool down the stream. I must have fallen asleep sometime last spring, maybe with the soft purr of the Farmall tractor, puttering up and down the long, monotonous rows in the potato field.

The sun's sleepy warmth helped too, and both the earth and I are now fully extended. The earth's soul is exhaled in summer, as ours is in sleep. Her breath is green, tinged with a rainbow of flowers. The aliveness above ground reflects a dearth of life below.

A neighbor drops by with a bushel of apples for us. He tries to remind me I grafted a Golden Sweet for him 15 years ago. Although I remember dreaming the trees I splice together every February will bear fruit someday, this connection remains intangible. It'll be autumn before I awaken.

Fall is when we bury cow horns stuffed with cow manure, which becomes potentized by its stay in the horn inside the earth's bosom while she is most alive. It's used as a spray or in compost tea and helps form a humus that has an inherent life of its own, eager to become a plant when a seed is sown. In the seed, we have an image of the whole universe, a miniature chaos, with a particular constellation taking effect. The life of the earth works on the plant as it grows, and eventually the lives of the community of people that support the farm are nourished.

Our last vegetable delivery is right before Christmas, and then the farm activities slow down a bit. At this time of year we can use our imagination to picture next year's garden, vibrant and healthy. We'll plan out the crop rotations, do concentration exercises for the problem areas, and simply think a little more broadly about the farm and its relationships.

Thinking often leads to wanting. Desires require natural resources to fulfill, and the farm offers a place where health, wealth and dreams are not only preserved, but revered and enhanced. We need a few things from the outer world today, fuel for the tractor and ice cream for an apple pie, which conjure up dreams of biodiesel and a new milk cow. When I go to town I feel many other forces at work on me, but here on the farm I'm much more in control, as if the dream is lucid.

As I wander down the verdant garden aisles, I sense the earth beneath my feet is sleeping. This display of exuberant photosynthesis will still be with us next winter, as a potential life force in the soil. Winter is the season when the earth inhales her life and soul back inside. The leaves will fall and bare branches, like outstretched nerve endings, will reveal limestone bluffs and distant horizons.

When the earth, and I, wake back up, new dreams will sprout.

December 16, 2003 (Written in late July)

I Can

I think, therefore I can. Amidst the abundant summer harvest, I consider our winter provisions. A peek in the cellar revealed empty shelves, and the Blue Lake beans were perfect. After sending 12 bushels of beans to Nashville, we picked two more for ourselves. With many helping hands, the beans are snapped, rinsed and set on the stove to boil. Quart jars are washed. I'm figuring a canner load of seven for every 1/2 bushel. While the beans are boiling, jars are scalded, and the lids are immersed in boiling water. I add a teaspoon of salt to each jar and fill them with hot beans and water to 1/4" from the top. Everything is hot. The top of the jar gets wiped clean, the lid screwed on, and they are set in a pressure canner.

All of the low-acid vegetables are canned in a pressure canner at 240 degrees, which is 10 pounds of pressure. My mom canned a lot and so have I, but I still like to look at the old, worn-out Ball Blue Book. It has all of the useful information you need, plus step-by-step instructions and many recipes.

Green beans are ready after 25 minutes at 10 pounds pressure. After the canner is taken off the stove, more jars are scalded, filled and sealed. When the pressure is down to zero, I take off the canner lid, but let it sit on top for a few minutes so cooler air doesn't rush in and break a jar. Canner tongs remove the completed jars and set the new ones in.

A fine pickle I've gotten myself into. With 20 bushels of cucumbers each week it was obvious what needed to happen. We grow Kirby cucumbers, the short, squat ones for pickling. The smaller ones are sorted out after washing, making for a nice break on the couch. Then it's busy-beaver time. Each jar gets a grape leaf, which has alum in it, and helps keep the pickle crisp. We get all of the ingredients out and wash the jars and lids.

The brine is a ½ gallon of water, ½ gallon of apple cider vinegar, and one cup of salt. The cukes are packed in scalded jars whole or sliced, and then we add a teaspoon of dill seed, ½ teaspoon of black peppercorns, and a few cloves of garlic. After sealing with the hot lids, we put them in a water bath for 10 minutes in a large kettle of boiling water. When they come out they sing, "ping, ping, ping," and we know they're sealed. Bread and butter pickles are made with no dill or garlic, but onions, celery seed, mustard seed, turmeric, ginger and sugar.

Grey mold is creeping through the tomato patch and will diminish the harvest. As we load the van on Monday, my workers pull out a few bushels of the dead ripe ones. "You're canning today," they inform me. "Get it while you can."

So, I pull out the bad ones and wash the good ones as water begins to boil. They're dipped in the boiling water until the skins slip, then plunged into cold water. Cored and skinned, they're back in a pot to cook down. A ½ bushel of peppers are cut up, along with a peck of onions, and added to about two bushels of tomatoes. I put some in smaller pans to cook down faster, and for the last 10 minutes a large bunch of sweet basil is immersed in the sauce. Eventually, they are in jars and water-bathed for 30 minutes. When I open them later, I will add garlic and oregano to go Italian, or hot peppers and cumin for a Mexican meal.

All of this takes hours, and often goes on till midnight. The labor is not hard, but beginning the daunting task requires commitment to finish it. I'm reminded of the children's book about the little red engine trying to climb the hill, over and over he says, "I think I can, I think I can."

August 4th, 2009

Buddhism

Last week, we were fortunate enough to get to hear a couple of Buddhist monks give a lecture. They were brothers who had escaped from Tibet when the Chinese invade in 1959. Their talk was about bringing the spiritual into our daily lives. The elder brother spoke in their native language and the younger one translated. They said the natural state of people is to be joyful and harmonious. All people are similar in that they want to be happy. We all share this goal.

Through our daily activities and interaction, unpleasant thoughts and emotions arise, which diminish our joy and happiness. Again, we all think and feel these emotions. They act like poisons to us. Anger, attachment and ignorance are the main culprits, but also jealousy and arrogance. Let's look at them closely.

When anger arises in us we often do something we will later regret. It is not good to let anger guide us. Many things make us angry, and it's natural for us to feel anger. But we can learn to let the anger go, and then deal with the cause of it from an anger-free state of mind.

Attachment is the most difficult. We are all attached to our loved ones, our homes and our possessions. We feel threatened when these attachments are not secure. Eventually, we will lose them anyway because we will die. Contemplating our own death is one way to loosen the hold our attachments have on us. Our happiness is not dependent on these things; it comes from inside us. How often have we really desired something, but then, after finally getting it, find we want something else?

Ignorance is a relatively easy one. Only after we've acquired knowledge do we need to remember to use it. But if we are ignorant, it is really not our fault. Our job is to be open to new ideas and to share our knowledge with those who are still learning. We all know things others don't and vice-versa. Communication, open-mindedness and mindfulness will go a long way towards eradicating ignorance.

Both jealousy and arrogance are related to attachment. In the former, we are afraid of losing something, or envious of what someone else has. Pridefulness is the surest way to unhappiness, because nothing lasts forever. All attachments are transitory.

So, how do we deal with these poisons? By cultivating the natural state of humans, which is joyfulness, love, compassion and kindness. These virtues will conquer the poisons every time. By being kind and compassionate we not only make others happy, we make ourselves happy.

Buddhists recommend meditation, or thinking very deeply about something. The monks suggested meditating on the feelings of love. We all love something in our lives: our parents, children, mates, friends or pets. Think about this feeling of love for a while, and let it grow to encompass the neighbors, the community, the country and then the world. Love is powerful and healing. When you feel the negative emotions, close your eyes and concentrate all of your attention on love and compassion for 5 or 10 minutes.

There is a lot of suffering in the world. You don't have to go far to see it. We can help alleviate suffering by replacing the poisons that arise in us with compassion and loving kindness. The people around us are just like us, confused and unhappy sometimes. They want to be happy. A kind act or compassionate word can go a long way.

I felt good after leaving the lecture hall, but it didn't take long to slip back into unkind thoughts. Negative emotions and feelings of arrogance, attachment and anger arise within me. I am just another human and suffer from these as much as anyone. But it was good to watch them arise, to step back, and look at myself as if holding up a mirror. I guess that's how we learn and change.

The spiritual is not a pie in the sky, a Sunday morning, or something we find later. The spiritual is kindness, compassion, joyfulness and love. When we bring these qualities into our daily lives we are being spiritual. The essence of Buddhism, as I understand it from the lecture I heard, seems to embrace Christianity wholeheartedly. When we face the trials of each day with compassion and loving kindness, and go about our business with joyful effort, we bring the world a little closer to peace.

November 6th, 2001

Christianity

Why does a farmer like to look at cows? What is it about a pastoral scene that is so comforting? How did the domestication of animals affect the history of civilization? What role will livestock play in the farms of tomorrow?

I always seem to wax philosophical as late autumn turns to early winter. Maybe it's the long nights with their Christmas lights, or the time spent feeding the cattle. As we ponder the mysterious and awesome life around us this time of year, with limestone bluffs peeking out from their summer cover, the creeks running full again, and the crackling fires cutting the chill from our cabins, our thoughts fall on a baby born in a manger.

Love, hope, faith, and forgiveness are continuously rekindled in the hearts of humanity by the deeds of this baby. The contemplation of these virtues leads us to acts of kindness and compassion for our fellow citizens. Two thousand years ago, the seeds were born for many of the world's great religions, Christianity and Islam included. From the Christian saints, reformers and crusaders to the Catholic Pope and the followers of Islam, all follow the teachings of Christ.

What does this have to do with cows, you may be wondering? Cattle connect us to the earth. We wouldn't be here without domestic animals because only they have provided the fertility and structure to the soil which sustains us. All of the great churches and mosques were built by humans living off animal products. Without the goats, sheep and cows our ancestors domesticated, there would be no civilization as we know it. The Bible is a historical, agricultural testament.

These animals were the first beings to behold the baby in the manger, and rightly so. Only afterwards did the gold, frankincense and myrrh appear with the kings. The gifts came after the gentle calmness and peace in the barnyard scene.

Today, we still feel a special warmth when we observe cattle contentedly munching on the rolling green pastureland. Deep in our subconsciousness, we know the foundation of our lives, the soil, is benefiting from the scene we are observing. The "holy cow" is aptly named indeed.

On the other hand, a sickening, repulsive feeling floods us when we see confined, crowded animals wallowing in their own wastes, or the miles of endless mono-cropland with no life-giving animals or trees around. A part of us knows it is not right to keep animals off the farmland, or to have farmland without animals and forests nearby.

My cows are starting to moo for hay. As I go about my fencing project, they are letting me know it's Christmas time, time to bring out a little of last summer's grass in the form of a sweet roll of hay. They don't seem to notice the missing calf, sacrificed to no longer serve us as a farm soil builder, but to be served as a human body builder at Christmas time.

How will I ever attain the Christ-consciousness to regard my fellow humans' welfare above my own? As much as I love cows, I've never seen them scoot over and let another cow have the best munch of hay. No, it's only the humans, whose lives the domestic animals make possible, that can develop compassion and love for others.

Gifts are great to give and to receive. But nothing is greater than the presence of the feeling of treating others better than ourselves, and nothing is harder to come by. As we sink into the deep winter, with Mother Nature fast asleep, our soul life awakens a little more, and we celebrate our role model's birthday. We feed our cows, they feed our soil, and us, but only our love for others feeds our soul.

Peace on Earth and Goodwill towards Men.

December 18th, 2001

Bell's Bend

Section I

Our mission is to grow high quality organic produce, and help others do the same. Many problems inherent in modern agricultural production disappear by farming organically on a smaller scale. Locally grown food uses less energy, and provides more employment. Soils are better cared for, and the farmers and surrounding environment are safer. There is reason to believe our nation's health crisis is directly related to an unhealthy food production and distribution system, such as factory farms and fast food. Another advantage of small farms is their beauty. They provide places for recreation, education and inspiration. Communities form around local family farms, enjoying good food and the fellowship that follows the food. Time and again I've spoken for the small, organic farm and against urban development, probably because the small farm where I was raised is now a subdivision.

As so often happens, I've spoken so much that I've put my foot in my mouth. A group of concerned citizens has asked me for my help in starting small organic farms in an effort to grow local food in an area threatened by development. The area, called Bell's Bend, has about 150 residents on approximately 8000 acres of beautiful farmland. The proposed development would bring in thousands of people in new homes, shopping malls and high rise buildings. Bell's Bend is just across the Cumberland River from Nashville, TN. Over the past 15 years, this community has banded together and fought off a proposed landfill, a sewage treatment plant, road widening and other urban development projects. They want to do something positive to show good reasons why their place should remain rural.

Having small organic farms for a model of alternative development is their dream.

Although located only 15 minutes from downtown Nashville, Bell's Bend feels like Macon County countryside. The farms are underutilized with old barns and a few cows. Many of the people I met had land and a vision, but no clue how to farm.

It is all there: manure piles, good soil, big and small tractors, hay for mulch, and close proximity to a million hungry people. Nashville could get good food from Bell's Bend farms, employing a large workforce to grow and process the produce. The organic food industry is booming, and the economy of local farms is booming. I've been under pressure to grow more produce at my place, but I like my size the way it is. While I can't just up and leave my farm, this project fits in with my overall mission - to grow high quality organic produce and help others do the same.

December 30th, 2008

Section II

I finally got a job, and it's right up my alley. I'm managing four new biodynamic gardens in the Bell's Bend neighborhood, near Nashville. A tight-knit group of conscientious folks have banded together in an effort to keep their community rural and clean, and their next step is to feed themselves. We're going to grow a few acres of vegetables.

The first farm is at George's, and this is where you can see whooping cranes. Two of less than 400 of the known wild ones make their nest on his farm. The soil is plowed, and we've put on horn manure and barrel compost, along with compost tea. 20 tons of biodynamic compost sit next to it, and this will fertilize half of an acre of potatoes and onions. We call it the "Whooping Crane Garden".

George's niece, Ellen, lives in the old family farmhouse nearby, and really wants a garden, too. The soil looks great, except for one problem – Johnson grass. I begged off, it would be too much to take on a garden infested by this pesky weed. She protested, implored, and prevailed. I agreed to grow watermelons on black plastic there, along with a berry patch. It will be on a quarter of an acre and is affectionately called "Ellen's Melons".

The main community garden is at Tom and Brenda's Sulfur Creek Farm. It is an acre divided into two sections. We're planning a garden shed, too. But I have my head buried in the soil.

Glynn brought many dump truck loads of halfway-rotted manure and bedding to the site. Other neighbors donated more finished manure composts. I put biodynamic preparations in it at once. Bill donated a pile of five-year-old wood chips that were well on the way to becoming humus. I decided to mix it all up.

Tom's tractor is small, without power steering. I am slowly making the compost piles when neighbor Zach brings a load of old manure from next door, which I had amended with preparations about a month earlier. I get off the tractor to thank him. "That medicine really seemed to help the manure rot," he said. I offered to put some in the fresh pile he had made. But I couldn't visit. I had way more work to do than time to do it. While I was back on the tractor, imagine my surprise, and joy, when he comes back, unasked, with a big backhoe. He saved me four hours of work, if not six.

The next morning, after putting preparations in over 100 tons of compost (plus Zach's new pile), we had a meeting. George is the only farmer in the gang, and we both agreed it was the day to chisel plow the garden. We have to expose the Bermuda grass to some freezing weather. So we talked awhile, and George simply gets up and leaves. When he comes back with the tractor I help him hook it up and he is off. After plowing lengthwise, we decide to hit it crossways, too.

Besides 100 tons of compost, I also needed a fence to keep the deer out. We took the property line fence down between Tom and George, and built the deer fence around both fields, with the line going right through the garden. Many neighbors donated posts and helped build the fence, and a sign at the garden entrance reads, "Good neighbors make good fences."

Joe is disappointed we aren't growing on his land. Glynn offers manure, so we'll plow and plant a corn patch there. We stir more horn manure and put it out with more compost tea. I want our vegetables to grow in a live soil humus, so there is a lot of focus on compost and tea right now.

What a community spirit! These folks all know each other and help each other out. Before their project, Tom, George, Zach and many of the neighbors didn't know each other very well. I spent time visiting folks and shooting the breeze at the local diner. Long lasting friendships were kindled, and the community building is extremely rewarding for everyone involved, although nobody thinks I'll be able to grow anything in those fields of Bermuda grass. Jim's taking pictures to document the garden, Kathleen is taking notes and organizing, and Eric and Louisa are ready to help hoe and harvest.

With daylight slipping fast, I get ready to drive the tractor to a different farm. I don't really have time, but I need to make compost over there. Devinder pulls up, and I'm too busy to visit. Next thing you know we are in his truck, getting a trailer, pulling the tractor to the other farm, and I finish the piles by 6:30. Everyone wants to help. We'll see who's out there when the rows of cucumbers, beans, and tomatoes need picking.

February 17th, 2009

Section III

In between the flurry of farm activities here, I slip into Davidson County and continue the fun. Twice we've taken our manure spreader there, and have about 100 tons of biodynamic compost spread over a little less than two acres on four different farms. One field is potatoes, one is sweet corn, one is melons and fruit, and the largest one is for the vegetable garden.

This is new land for me, new tractors, and new people, so I am definitely on a learning curve. On the day I arrived to plant potatoes, George informed me that there was a wet-weather spring in the back third of the field. But they already had the seed potatoes cut up, so we planted the whole patch. With the extra wet weather, that part of the field did not come up. So our potato crop, which is flowering and hilled, will be less than we planned. But I planned on too much anyway, so we are about on target.

Ellen's melons and fruit farm is full of Johnson grass. So it is covered with a woven ground cloth and has blackberries planted. On the lower side, we made hills with compost, and planted watermelons and cantaloupes. This was covered with black plastic, and holes a foot in diameter were cut over the hills. Lots of rocks and wood were laid on to help keep the plastic from flying away.

Three rows of tomatoes start out the Sulfur Creek garden, followed by alternating rows of vining plants and quick maturing crops. We'll harvest the latter about the time the vines take over. Two rows of pole beans will add visual flavor, along with a row each of zinnias and cosmos.

Part of what we're doing in this project is helping younger folks experience gardening. It drives me nuts. On a freshly plowed patch, five "apprentices" were tromping around pulling up crabgrass roots. They were in the wrong place, and I called them a herd of elephants, because each footprint sank down four inches in the fluffy soil. I wish I was nicer, but packed garden soil makes me cringe.

As I watched them transplant lettuce, I knew I should teach them how to do it efficiently. They were going slow, planting too deep, and still tromping too much. So I get off the tractor and demonstrate, in my abrupt, egotistical manner. Smooth the soil evenly, someone hands me six plants, I set them and then shift myself forward and plant six more. I am so fast and good, I plant a hundred row feet in the time they could plant ten.

That's when I realized I'd planted the wrong furrow, and had to dig them all up and replant. How do people put up with me? Three 400-foot rows of summer squash, three of beans and two of cucumbers will require help during harvest, so I hope I didn't scare anyone away. We finished the day planting the sweet corn patch, and it was a blessing to have eight extra hands. The biodynamic humus-forming preparations were applied at sunset. Altogether, we have used 32 sets of the compost preparations, and put horn manure and barrel compost on the fields 18 times.

Horn silica was sprinkled on in the morning along with fermented horsetail tea, and then more gardens were planted. We have ulterior motives in Bell's Bend. Developers want to build a bridge across the Cumberland River and bring in another downtown there, and these folks don't want it. To "keep Bell's Bend country," they are fighting for their rural lifestyle in the planning commissioner's meetings. A visible presence of organic food production is my role.

A few thousand acres are at stake. It could be the breadbasket of Nashville, supplying fresh produce, creating local jobs, and preserving the environment. Or, 50,000 people could move in, high rise apartments and shopping centers could go up, and the area becomes "developed." We hope to "develop" it into organic farms and gardens instead.

June 6th, 2009

Addendum from Early 2011

By the end of the 2009 season, the Bell's Bend farms had grossed $25,000 off a little more than an acre-and-a-half of gardens. They were featured in many articles, on TV, and have hosted thousands of visitors. The vibrant community of young people hanging out and learning gardening there prompted me to apologize to the owners for starting a commune on their land. Two years later, they are still going strong. Eric has bought a couple of tractors, and Bell's Bend is noted for its beautiful biodynamic gardens. Urban development is on hold.

A similar project I did in 2010 was at the Glen Leven Estate with Tyler Brown, the chef at the Hermitage Hotel restaurant. At the end of that year, he said his restaurant used $15,000 of produce from the one-acre garden. He has also bought a couple of tractors, and that garden continues to thrive.

Extension Agent

I am a biodynamic farm extension agent, visiting organic gardens and farms and offering advice. This was not planned. It just happens that many gardens are sprouting up to meet the demand for local produce, and I've been a local market gardener for 30 years. If someone with 30 years of experience in organic growing in Tennessee had visited me when I started, they could have saved me 20 years of mistakes. Well, only if I had listened and taken their advice, which is doubtful. I had read books and knew everything by the time I was 25. It took many years to realize how little I do know. So how can I help others?

I answer questions, based on my observations of their gardens and my own similar situations. I want to know how the nitrogen and carbon cycles are managed, what equipment is used, the quantities of lime applied, and what the compost looks, feels and smells like. I'm interested and fascinated by gardens.

Every farm is unique, and reflects the intentions of the farmer. Most of the "farmers" I meet are new to it. Accounting, law, and psychiatry are among the professions the folks I've met have given up to become farmers. They're very intelligent people. But farming requires something more important than intelligence. Farmers have what's called common sense, and you can't get it by reading books or surfing on the internet. It is transmittable with farmer to farmer contact.

My dad was a farmer, and from him I learned when to plow, how to use a hoe and what to put in a compost pile. But he didn't know that Tennessee gardens need extra lime, or how to loosen up heavy clay soil. He farmed in the rich soils of Illinois. My neighbors taught me a lot about farming locally.

Visiting other farms has been extremely educational for me. I learn about techniques, tools and varieties I've heard about but never ran into. I try to remain open minded, which is hard to do because I'm so opinionated. Still, it's a useful challenge to try and understand how a person manages their land.

My biodynamic advisory service puts the primary focus on soil health. I farm like old timers, so I want to know why folks deviate from the way people have always grown food. A grade school textbook on farming that's a hundred years old clearly explains most of what I do.

A few extra volunteers on our farm allow me a little extra time, and they also learn by visiting other farms. I've been given much information over the years, and want to continue the tradition of passing along anecdotal knowledge. Maybe I can shorten for others the long learning curve I undertook several decades ago, and in the process acquire more new ideas.

July 21st, 2009

Farm Festival

It was a busy late September, as we once again turned the cabin into a conference center. The living room became a dining hall and lecture room, and the whole house got a good cleaning. Pumpkins and gourds dotted the corners of the yard and an outdoor kitchen materialized.

Old friends started arriving and setting up their campsites. New bracing for the barn loft floor got done in time for major decorating. Kids began playing, and the cooks kept cooking. Here we go again.

Alan Savory's holistic management relies on the proper utilization of pastureland, and Greg covered it superbly. Richard and David were talking about bees in another three-hour workshop, when I realized I'd forgotten to collect seven buckets of manure. I interrupted everyone and organized an impromptu farm tour. As that's where the cows and bees were, everyone agreed, and off we went.

The Friday night banquet featured eggplant parmesan, salads, greens, potatoes, and pumpkin pies. Almost everything we ate all weekend was homegrown and delicious. These conferences are not about lectures on farming; they are about eating farm-fresh food. Our surprise guest of honor Friday night was Crazy Owl, our local 83 year old herbalist, and the bonfire became an oyster roast.

Saturday began with talks on radionics, beekeeping, nature spirits, calcium and silica, the biodynamic preparations and the plants used to make them, and the garden I started for a Nashville restaurant. After a huge lunch, we experienced homeopathy, minerals for health, anthroposophical medicine, compost tea, bio-char, homemade jam and mustard, and the spiritual hierarchies. I continued to keep horn-stuffing going, and we made a batch of barrel compost.

Young kids bounced all over the place, and many young adults were itching to bounce. Another feast was followed by the long anticipated talent show. We saw skits and tricks, songs and dance, hula-hooping and poetry reading. The big bonfire lent excitement, all leading up to a rock 'n' roll barn dance. The break dancing was unbelievable; it was biodynamics at its best.

We picked up all the pieces Sunday morning and had our "Church." This is when we read from the Agriculture Course, and the lecture was number four. We studied why in the world we would stuff a cow horn with manure. All who wanted some were encouraged to take home horn manure, horn silica, and barrel compost at no cost.

A tent was set up for trading, and the JPI (Josephine Porter Institute) bookshop was a hit. Honey, jam, and a few other goodies were also available. And the children kept playing.

Our last workshops were about interns. A circle formed and everyone was either a farm with interns or an intern. Everybody spoke in turn. A need arose for more connection in our Southeastern biodynamic association with these two groups of people. Although each farm has unique intern dynamics, the uniqueness of each farm can be nothing but valuable for those wanting to learn. We hope to move interns from farm to farm in our area on a more regular basis.

In 1982 I helped start the Tennessee Alternative Growers Association (we avoided the word "organic" back then because it had a negative connotation in the mainstream media). I was active in planning organic conferences in the 1980's and 1990's. In 1987, we started an annual biodynamic conference in Georgia, which moved to my cabin in 1996. Within a few years, it was no longer just a conference for the Southeastern biodynamic association, it was a harvest festival. It has further evolved into the annual biodynamic family reunion.

Long hugs and loving goodbyes were Sunday afternoon's activities, followed by a small candlelight dinner of leftovers. About 150 folks attended, and about 40 gave us enough money to cover expenses. Everyone pitched in where needed, doing dishes and chopping vegetables. A big thank you to all who came, especially the vibrant youngsters. "With our agricultural conference we have also enjoyed a real farm festival" (R. Steiner), is as true today as it was in 1924.

October 26th, 2010

S.S.A.

The School for Sustainable Agriculture is the name of our farm's apprenticeship program, and the acronym clearly expresses how we do everything here. The staff of two have 50 years of combined farming failures to provide interns with a steady supply of amusement. The curriculum includes monotonous farm work interspersed with the bioneurotic farmer's rambling, ranting, and raving, and the silence of the zany zen gardener. Interns teach as well as try to learn something from these two.

A steady stream of family, friends and neighbors routinely interrupt the hectic days, so nothing ever goes as planned. On Mondays and Thursdays, the delivery van is crammed full of vegetables. The rest of the week we spend doing what didn't get done last week, repairing what just broke, or trying to locate lost tools. The fields are hot and buggy, the woods are full of poison ivy and ticks, and most of the snakes are not poisonous.

A herd of scrawny, unmanaged cattle roam various meadows searching for edible forage. One hundred and fifty rolls of weedy hay fed to them during the winter make a manure mess that's turned into compost for the five acres of vegetables. The farmer does weird things with herbs and animal organs in attempts to benefit microbial population explosions as well as to strengthen imponderable forces.

Lodging consists of a room in the overcrowded intern cabin, your tent or the barn loft. There is an outdoor kitchen, an outhouse, and a creek for washing in. Interns are welcome to pester the farmer for hot showers, meals or a ride into town.

Food is plentiful – all the potatoes and kale you can eat. If you go hungry, it's your fault. There are lots of gardens and even more weeds, many of which are edible.

As farmers, we don many hats, the fool's cap being the most common. Our carpentry crew, Crowbar Construction, goes by the motto, "Why do it right the first time when you can rush now and get to do it again soon?" The Red Knuckle mechanics are still trying to learn "lefty loosie," "righty tighty" and would rather do other things under the shade tree. As accountants ,we rely heavily on trash cans and good luck. The music parties happen at the drop of a hat, and our hats fall off frequently.

There are no classes or schedules, and you can pretty much do what you like. It's a self study program, so bring a mirror. The best way to help us is often just staying out of the way. You'll have access to the farmer's library of Steiner stuff and old agricultural textbooks, though he'll want you to read his own book first, in an effort to avoid the Department of Redundancy department.

The farm accepts no grant money, not that anyone would give us any anyway. Our meager income comes from what we do on the farm, so we can't offer you a stipend. We charge nothing for your stay and you'll soon see why. Interns get the most menial jobs and are lucky to catch fleeting glimpses of the hairy, harried farmers trying vainly to get their work done. We raise about 100,000 pounds of produce each year, and love help hauling it around. Despite the thorns and chiggers, lessons and lectures, and the sweat and sore muscles, many graduates of the S.S.A. end up becoming farmers.

Our educational aim is for you to breathe deeply and sleep well, and to be filled with wonder and interest for this beautiful world. If you'd like to enroll, you can try to call us – we occasionally answer the phone. The farmer has email, but doesn't know how to use a computer, so snail mail is much quicker. Drop by anytime and try to find us, we're around here somewhere and will come stumbling home sooner or later.

November 15th, 2005

We Can

We can grow most of our own food in home gardens and on small farms. Agriculture before the 20th century depended upon healthy soil. Farmers knew how to keep their soils capable of long term production. All farms had animals for power and food, and the waste products were composted to keep the land fertile. Crops were grown in rotation so they didn't wear out the soil, and cover crops were grown to enrich the land. Everyone that needed a job had one. Gardening was common and 'putting food up' was simply a part of life. Our nation became strong and independent through agriculture. I've studied USDA publications from the early 1900's and find them excellent sources of information.

Great improvements occurred in agriculture during this period. People were anxious to learn all they could about how plants grew. Country folk sent their kids to college to learn from the "experts." Justus von Leibig's early experiments were especially important. He demonstrated the plant's need for nitrogen, phosphorus and potassium, and found that materials used for gunpowder supplied these nutrients. He also confirmed the need for soil to have adequate humus, but this fact was later ignored.

During the first half of the 20th century, two world wars happened which further strengthened the power of the United States. Most of the weapons used in these wars, by both sides, were made and sold by the same manufacturers. After the First World War, the weapons industry started selling their wares for fertilizer rather than weapons. It was hard to sell it. Farmers didn't need it, because years of wise care had kept their farms fertile. Although it did increase yields, fertilizer was only used in conjunction with manure. It was even called "artificial manure."

The United States Department of Agriculture (the USDA) started recommending that farmers either grow animals or crops, but not both, and that they use these chemicals even though they destroyed soil humus. Their policies have had a tremendous effect on farming in our country, and their funding goes to further the research at land grant colleges. The way most farms operate is a direct result of the information the USDA disseminates through their various programs.

After World War II, there was a huge increase in the industry's push to sell fertilizer. When the soil's humus became depleted, the same companies sold pesticides for the inevitable insect and disease pressure that attend crops grown without humus. These chemical/weapon/fertilizer companies also funded the land grant colleges, who did the research on their products. They are the giant grain cartels and food processors. The results of the research were that farmers should buy what they were selling.

By the 1970's the USDA's official standpoint was "get big or get out," and "take out fences and hedgerows," which paved the way for a total separation of animal husbandry from crop production. Through their incentive programs, most farm animals are now raised in confinement operations, and most cropland is inundated with chemicals.

At this time about 3000 farmers, calling themselves "organic," began doing their own research. They rediscovered pre-chemical era techniques that built soil humus and allowed for continuous crop production without a lot of inputs. This handful of farmers, of which I was one, also formed sustainable agriculture groups across the country and held conferences and workshops. More importantly, they developed markets for organic food and consequently the whole organic food movement. During the next 20 years, the USDA totally ignored organics and continued promoting chemical use in agriculture.

In 1990, Congress passed an act demanding that the USDA fund organic research, conferences and marketing. We thought this was great, finally getting recognition for our efforts. Little did we know how tricky these corporations can be. The USDA and the huge agricultural companies are the same people, simply switching jobs occasionally.

It's only my opinion, but I question if the organic movement was helped by the last 20 years of the USDA's funding, which is a tiny fraction of their total budget. Their research is product-oriented, not about self-sufficient agriculture that doesn't need off-farm inputs. Big agribusiness is not being challenged to return livestock to the farms, to stop using chemicals and genetically-engineered organisms, or to rebuild our nation's soil.

I feel the integrity of organics has gone downhill in the last 20 years with their "certification" and "marketing." But it's the USDA sponsored "sustainable" conferences at fancy hotels and convention centers, complete with corporate "food" (a real slap in the face), that drew my attention to how our movement has been usurped by big agribusiness. If we follow the money trail, it is apparent who the USDA wants to help and how they marginalize organics.

Organic farmers do great research on their own and are having wonderful conferences on farms with their own food and speakers. CSA's associate and collaborate for mutually beneficial relationships between farmers and consumers. The huge movement of conscious people making a change in American agriculture excites me, especially the amount of young people getting involved. If the USDA food programs in schools, prisons, hospitals, and welfare change to organic, then many of our country's abandoned farms and rural ghost towns will spring to life. When folks refuse corporate food, small farms will sprout and food will be abundant. Gardens can be easily grown, and there will be no lack of good things to eat.

I not only think we can feed ourselves and each other, I know we can.

February 2nd, 2010

Compost Blues

When I die and you lay me down
Call all my friends around
But don't drop me six feet underground
Put me in a compost pile
Put me in a compost pile
Be sure to be wearing a smile
When I go meet my maker
I won't need no undertaker
Put me in a compost pile
I believe that would be my style
One fine day I will be free
Finally know what that will be
And you will finally know what to do with me
Bury me up to my earlobes
Need to feed my soil microbes
Put me in a compost pile
Watch what grows up in a little while

www.ingramcontent.com/pod-product-compliance
Lightning Source LLC
Chambersburg PA
CBHW071959290426
44109CB00018B/2072